Solving the Post Traumatic Stress Brain Injury Puzzle

A First Responder's GPS

Linda Green BS, CHPC

1st Edition, 1st printing 2019.

Cover design by Steve Walters at Oxygen Publishing House, www.oxygenpublishing.com
Interior design by Steve Walters at Oxygen Publishing House
Cover illustration by Steve Walters at Oxygen Publishing House
Interior illustrations by Brendan Wright
Author photo by Bob Minenna

ISBN-13: 978-1724878816 (CreateSpace-Assigned)
ISBN-10: 1724878816

TABLE OF CONTENTS

Glossary Of Terms

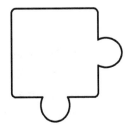

Automatic Negative Thoughts

Surface level, non-volitional, stream of consciousness that appears in the form of descriptions, inferences, or situation specific evaluations. Reflexive reactions. Based on beliefs people hold about themselves. A negative bias towards self.

California Department of Forestry and Fire Protection (CAL FIRE)

The men and women of the California Department of Forestry and Fire Protection (CAL FIRE) are dedicated to the fire protection and stewardship of over 31 million acres of California's privately-owned wildlands. In addition, the Department provides varied emergency services in 36 of the State's 58 counties via contracts with local governments.

Computer Aided Dispatching (CAD)

Computer-aided dispatch (CAD) is a method of dispatching emergency services assisted by computer. It can either be used to send messages to the responding unit via a mobile data terminal and/or used to store and retrieve data (i.e. radio logs, field interviews, client information, schedules, etc.). A dispatcher may announce the call details to field units over a two-way radio. Some systems communicate using a two-way radio system's selective calling features. CAD systems may send text messages with call-for-service details to alphanumeric pagers or wireless text services like SMS.

Conflagration

A conflagration is a large and destructive fire that threatens human life, animal life, health, and/or property. It may also be described as a blaze or simply a (large) fire. A conflagration can begin accidentally (improper wiring), be naturally caused (lightning), or intentionally created (arson).

Critical Incident Stress Management (CISM)

An intervention protocol developed specifically for dealing with traumatic events. It is a formal, highly structured and professionally recognized process for helping those involved in a critical incident to share their experiences, vent emotions, learn about stress reactions and symptoms and given referral for further help if required. It is not psychotherapy. It is a confidential, voluntary and educative process, sometimes called 'psychological first aid'.

First developed for use with military combat veterans and then civilian responders (police, fire, EMS, emergency workers and disaster rescuers) it has now been adapted and used virtually everywhere there is a need to address traumatic events in people's lives.

Dissociation

Dissociation is a mental process that causes a lack of connection in a person's thoughts, memory and sense of identity. Dissociation seems to fall on a continuum of severity. Mild dissociation would be like daydreaming, getting "lost" in a book, or when you are driving down a familiar stretch of road and realize that you do not remember the last several miles. A severe and more chronic form of disso-

ciation is seen in the disorder Dissociative Identity Disorder

Emergency Responder Exhaustion Syndrome (ERES)

A psychoeducational format using everyday language to assist first responders and their families understand their reactions to cumulative and critical incident stress. The four key components of ERES include anger, isolation, depression, and exhaustion.

Eye Movement Desensitization and Reprocessing (EMDR)

EMDR therapy is an integrative psychotherapy approach that has been extensively researched and proven effective for the treatment of trauma. EMDR is a set of standardized protocols that incorporates elements from many different treatment approaches.

FIRESCOPE

The FIRESCOPE program originated in Southern California, organized under the acronym, "FIrefighting REsources of Southern California Organized for Potential Emergencies" in 1972. By legislative action, the FIRESCOPE Board of Directors and the Office of Emergency Services Fire and Rescue Service Advisory Committee were consolidated into a working partnership which represents all facets of local, rural, and metropolitan fire departments, the California Department of Forestry and Fire Protection, and federal fire agencies.

Foehn winds

A warm, dry and strong general wind that flows down into valleys when stable, high pressure air is forced across and then down the lee slopes of a mountain range. The descending air is warmed and dried due to adiabatic compression producing critical fire weather conditions. Locally called be various names in California including, Santa Ana winds, Devil winds, North winds, and Mono winds.

Lake County Community Radio (KPFZ 88.1 FM)

KPFZ broadcasts to Lake County and surrounding areas with over 50 different music and public affairs programs for all musical tastes and points of views. Provided critical local radio coverage during the Valley Fire, operating non-stop for weeks before resuming normal operations.

Leader's Intent

In fast-moving, dynamic situations, top-level decision makers cannot always incorporate new information into a formal planning process and redirect people to action within a reasonable timeframe. It allows people closest to the scene of action to adapt plans and exercise initiative to accomplish the objective when unanticipated opportunities arise or when the original plan no longer suffices.

Mammatus clouds

Mammatus clouds develop when moist air sinks into dry air due to a powerful downdraft which reverses the normal convective process. As updrafts bring precipitation-enriched air onto the top of the cloud, the upward force is lost, and the air starts to spread horizontally, eventually becoming part of the anvil cloud. Because the parcel of moist air is heavier than the nearby air, it sinks until it reaches the base of the anvil where moisture evaporates. However, the packets of wet air and ice crystals are large enough that evaporation cannot take place at the cloud base. These moist air parcels continue to sink further creating sac-like pouches.

"Office"

The "office" was a rented office space in Middletown, where I first started to work on this book. Conveniently located in the same building as the local coffee shop Mugshots. Not to be confused with the office I was paid to be at for CAL FIRE. I did the best I could to keep the two activities separated by both time and space.

Post-Traumatic Stress Disorder

Post-traumatic stress disorder (PTSD) is a psychiatric disorder that can occur in people who have experienced or witnessed a traumatic event such as a natural disaster, a serious accident, a terrorist act, war/combat, rape or other violent personal assault. People with PTSD have intense, disturbing thoughts and feelings related to their experience that last long after the traumatic event has ended. They may relive the event through flashbacks or nightmares; they may feel sadness, fear or anger; and they may feel detached or estranged from other people. People with PTSD may avoid situations or people that remind them of the traumatic event, and they may have strong negative reactions to something as ordinary as a loud noise or an accidental touch.

Stigma

A virtual or physical mark denoting disgrace, disapproval or disease, usually describing a person or a group. People with mental illnesses, for example, are stigmatized by employers and co-workers as being moody, unreliable, or erratic. Military veterans and first responders suffering from post-traumatic stress injuries frequently judge themselves harshly for their own perceived weaknesses, creating a type of self-imposed stigma.

Wildland Urban Interface (WUI)

Locations where structures and communities meet or intermingle with undeveloped wildland. In the US, over 46 million homes have been built in the WUI and are potentially at risk from WUI fire. (See NIST in Reference section)

Endorsements

Linda Green provides a behind the scenes look at how Post-Traumatic Stress impacted her life and the lives of those she loved. She takes a no-nonsense approach in shining a light on some of her thoughts, her judgements, and her actions as she has been moving forward in her life. A MUST READ for anyone experiencing PTS or knows someone who is!

Paul Gowin

High Performance Strategist

This is not just a book about PTSD. It is a way through!

Today we are surrounded with news and information and it can be overwhelming. Just think about the news. How often are 1st responders on a scene doing their job? More often than we realize. What we tend to focus on is their commitment, skills and courage. That is good. But what we tend to forget is that every time they are needed it is a trauma situation. They live on high alert and that makes them ready for the call but it also has consequences that are real and seldom talked about and worse dismissed.

Linda in writing this book has done several things: shined a real light on PTSD through her journey and provides a process for others to use to navigate through theirs and addresses the stigma and lack of understanding associated with trauma and PTSD. She also shines a light so others are more aware and can actually be more helpful and not do unintentional harm.

If you or a loved one is struggling, get this book and walk with the author through the process. She knows and has done it. Let her help you. You are not alone. I also recommend this book for leaders. We need to know so we can lead and not harm.

Thank you, Linda for stepping up and out and sharing this gift with the world!

Kimberly Allain
Founder, Allain Solutions

In this powerful firsthand account, Linda Green pulls the reader in with her honest and unvarnished retelling of her struggles with PTS and the reactions she encountered from the organization to which she devoted 32 years of her life. It tells how she forged her own path, determined to change her life and meet the daily ongoing challenges thrown at her. By extension, she guides us to our own understanding of what it's like to live with PTS and provides calls to action for both a community response and others who need help.

It's easy to admire Linda as she speaks out on a subject that too often gets swept under the rug by people who are uninformed, unaware or too afraid to deal with the aftermath of the ordeals suffered by coworkers, subordinates, family members or friends.

Reading through her entries will make you furious that good

people have to go through this.

Part narrative, part prescriptive and at times stunningly poetic, it can be hard to read since we know what is happening, but even harder to put down.

During a moment of reflection, Linda says that she is one of the lucky ones. In truth, we who have read her story are also the lucky ones.

Fairbourne Frye

MBA, CEO Insight Catalyst Coaching

Linda Green is a woman I love. And she's a woman that every firefighter, law enforcement officer, and EMS provider should come to know. And she's doing her part by writing this book.

You see, Assistant Chief (Ret.) Linda Green had a 32-year career with CAL Fire, a career that ended, not on her terms, but on the terms of PTSD (Post Traumatic Stress Disorder). When she was forced to leave the job she loved, it wasn't with the honor and respect anyone in a similar position would have expected.

Instead, she was another victim of the STIGMA, the stigma associated with those who struggle with behavioral and mental health issues and the inability of the organizations they work for to recognize the problems and help the individual seek meaningful treatment for their condition.

Now Linda Green could have curled up in a ball in a dark room for the rest of her life. Or she could have lost herself in a bottle. Or she could have become one of the growing number of firefighters, law enforcement officers, and EMS providers who take their own lives because they can't deal with the symptoms of PTSD and what's happening within their brain.

But she didn't. Instead she's written this book, a book that took me as the reader right into the middle of the firestorm that was Linda Green's brain. A book where she shares the journey of her struggles with PTSD on a daily, and sometimes hourly, basis.

A book that is destined to be a trailblazer in the world of PTSD and first responders because it will appeal to many different audiences: those suffering from post-traumatic stress; those who work with, supervise, or manage those individuals; and psychologists and other mental health professionals working with public safety personnel suffering from post-traumatic stress.

Why did she write this book? Part of it was the therapeutic value for her (Which is very much visible when you read her journal entries in the book), but the larger part is that she wanted other firefighters and her brother and sisters in law enforcement and EMS to learn from her own journey and struggles.

Why? Because she's a firefighter and that's what firefighters do.

Robert P. Avsec

Battalion Chief (retired), Chesterfield (Va.) Fire and EMS Department and Blogger-in-Chief at Talking "Shop" 4 Fire & EMS

INTRODUCTION

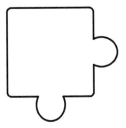

"I was blindsided. That's probably the best way to describe how it felt, as a perfect storm of forces was brewing, never before experienced by any of us, and descended it's wrath upon us that day... and changed everything." - Linda Green

September 12, 2015

Linda Green was the Incident Commander on the devastating Valley Fire that burned across 76,000 acres in the CAL FIRE Sonoma-Lake-Napa Unit, destroying almost 2000 structures and bringing upon us the heartbreak of lives lost. But in the months that followed the traumatic event she refers to as "her fire", she knew something was very wrong, even though life seemed to be marching on as always...until it wasn't. The nuances were there immediately but were masterfully disguised by her well-worn habits of performance and responsibility. She didn't yet realize her freefall had begun into her own personal "hellfire".

Linda was diagnosed with a Post-Traumatic Stress Injury just months before her retirement in 2016.

Like millions of First Responders who are called to serve on the front lines, she dedicated a 32-year career to the safety of others. She was now called to accept her most important mission yet; as a First Responder to herself. Her own Post-Traumatic Brain Injury diagnosis would become an intricate and confusing puzzle to solve, and she would need to find the courage to be curious and create a roadmap to recovery. She now shares this roadmap to teach others so they too can find the courage to be curious about solving their Post Traumatic Brain Injury puzzle too.

Throughout her own research and first-person recovery and healing, she now believes that Post-Traumatic Growth is a theory in dire need of awareness and attention as well as Emergency Response Exhaustion Syndrome. While Post-Traumatic Stress Disorder – PTSD – has been an accepted diagnosis since 1980, she is one of a growing number of leading experts in this field, who believe in its reclassification from Disorder to Injury.

Linda is now a Certified High Performance Coach who uses her strategic principles and wisdom to guide other First Responders pre and post diagnosis through the discovery and recovery process. Her journey continues to teach her that the only way to get back up is to grab hold of a hand that will reach out to you as you fall. It is her genuine hope that her book acts as that hand reaching out to anyone who needs it.

puz·zle [pəzəl/]

Verb

Cause (someone) to feel confused because they cannot understand or make sense of something

Synonym: perplex, confuse, bewilder, bemuse, baffle, mystify, confound

Noun

A game, toy, or problem designed to test ingenuity or knowledge

---

NOTE: Type in **BOLD PRINT** is a symptom of post-traumatic stress, as it manifested in my life.

Journal entries were written on the date noted so they are, in essence, my PTSD journey – in real time.

PREFACE

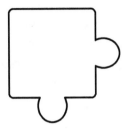

There is an ongoing discussion whether or not post-traumatic stress is a disorder (PTSD) or an injury (PTSI). Maybe it's a little bit of both. The long-term physical effect of post-traumatic stress coupled with the decreased functional ability of PTSI can be debilitating if not handled right. My personal experience with PTSI, the various therapies I engage in and all the reading I've done on the subject has led me to advocate that we update our understanding of it based on new studies, emerging research and neuroscience.

SIGNS AND SYMPTOMS

First responders have an opportunity to assist people in many ways. Emergency medical responses in the pre-hospital environment encompass everything from febrile seizures, to heart attacks and strokes, to traumatic physical injuries. Emergency medical technicians and paramedics are trained to provide limited diagnoses based on the signs and symptoms presented by the patient, so that they can initiate the appropriate level of care.

A sign is something that is objective, it can be measured, or it's visible. This would include things like a rash, that somebody else can see. A cough can be heard, a high temperature can be measured with a thermometer, blood pressure can be measured, viruses can be observed with a microscope, or broken bones can be visualized with x-rays. Those are all examples of signs - something that is objective because other people can see it or hear it or, in some way or another, it can be measured.

That's different from a symptom, which is much more subjective. It is something that is felt and described as it's being experienced by the person. Things like this would include something like a stomach ache, or back pain or fatigue. Those aren't necessarily things that can be measured, but the person experiencing them can describe them.

Symptoms can be chronic, relapsing or remitting/acute. Usually in the world of EMS we talk about chronic and acute quite a bit. Acute or remitting symptoms would be like symptoms of the common cold, you suffer with those for a little bit, and they pretty much take care of themselves, and they go away. Chronic symptoms, such as shortness of breath experienced by asthmatics, linger around for the long term. The severity is variable, but the symptoms are ever present. Then there are relapsing symptoms. People who live with anxiety and depression are familiar with these. There are good days and bad days, but these symptoms come and go.

Signs are objective but the experience of PTSI is subjective. It is hard to measure, diagnose and treat. The good news is that new studies are emerging on a regular basis. From these, new treatments are being developed so there is great hope for the future of PTS sufferers.

As for me, my experiences in the field, with the people who have both helped and hindered my progress in healing, and the research I have done have served to give my PTSI a voice. I will not hide nor will I allow it to diminish my life. On the contrary, it has been the gift that has redirected my life to serving others in a field that has redirected my life purpose. I invite you to join me on a journey through post-traumatic stress.

How To Use This Book

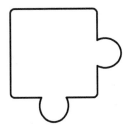

The vision for this book has transformed with every page written. Where it stands now is this. A post-traumatic stress injury (PTSI) is bad enough for anyone dealing with it. When First Responders, who are used to being in control, find their own behavior to be uncharacteristically out of control, a post-traumatic stress injury is just a double whammy. Both injured, and out of control. I don't know about you, but I thought I was going crazy until I was diagnosed with PTSI.

This book is for people who are struggling under the weight of a potential post-traumatic stress injury, but,

- Don't know who to ask
- Don't know what to ask
- Don't know why their spouse has changed so drastically
- Whose brain may be too on fire to make sense of scientific jargon
- Who find that a list of symptoms without context is meaningless
- Supervisors who don't understand why a top performer

suddenly can't get their act together

If this is you, you're in the right place.

This book is meant to be written in. I provided pages in the back to take notes on. There are journaling exercises to help create an individual pathway towards recovery.

Most importantly, as you go through this book, I identified how symptoms were showing up in my life. They are in BOLD print. As you go through the book, highlight the parts that apply to your own life. List them out in the back of the book.

If you haven't been diagnosed, take that list to your doctor and use it as a starting point to have a discussion about your symptoms.

Asking for help is not a weakness. It is a courageous act. So, please, ask for help.

Recovery is worth it.

Linda

SECTION 1

MY STORY

My First Responder Story

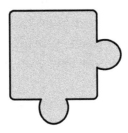

It started in High School, when I made the decision that I wanted to help people. At the time I didn't know what form that would take yet, but that was my decision.

My senior year in high school, a job announcement for the summer caught my attention: Seasonal Firefighter for the California Division of Forestry (CDF). Intrigued, I spoke with the school counselor, and then submitted my application. I was selected to attend the 40-hour academy, sponsored by the Fresno County Regional Occupational Program, and spent a three-day weekend in February at the Blasingame Forest Fire Station in Fresno County.

Three days after I graduated from high school, I put on a uniform and reported for duty. To say that it was easy from that point on would be a massive understatement. Unknowingly caught up in the politics of gender equality, my first captain thought I didn't belong, and sent my ass packing after I suffered a heat exhaustion injury. A week later I had my job back after my mom, a savvy union shop steward in her own right, interceded on my behalf. When I left for college a month later, I didn't know if I should go back.

That winter, after I gave a friend a ride up into the foothills so she could visit some friends, I stopped on the side of Highway 41 just south of Coarsegold. The stars were spectacular, unwashed by the city lights of Fresno. Inspired, I filed my paperwork for another summer, vowing to make the most of a second chance.

As the stars would have it, that summer I moved north to the Ahwahnee Forest Fire Station in Madera County. There I found the right combination of people to work with and learned the job the right way. By my third summer I was hooked and redirected my college studies towards a fire science degree. I took entry tests around the state, even though my ultimate goal was to land a job with CDF. My peers encouraged me along the way, and we had many a meal together after taking tests, as we were all chasing that brass ring of a career.

In 1985 I was promoted to Limited-Term (LT) Fire Apparatus Engineer. The LT academy was twelve days straight of classroom, driving, and pumping practice. Category A and B tests were clumped in towards the end of the class. Fail a Category A test, and you had one more shot at it. Otherwise, you were gone. Highly motivated, I passed all my tests and was given my new assignment in a new unit.

I headed north to Lake County and found myself attached to the Boggs Mountain Helitack Base. No fire engine for me that summer. I drove a stake-side truck, with four 55-gallon barrels of Jet A fuel strapped in the back, along with a Briggs & Stratton pump, miscellaneous tools, and a spare Bambi-bucket.

The area was not the hotbed of activity it is now, and it was six weeks before I ever pumped fuel into the A-Star 350-D helicopter on a working fire. By Labor Day, the county had received over two inches of rain, and I was let go for the year.

With the new year of 1986, came a new opportunity. This time, a permanent assignment as a Fire Apparatus Engineer (FAE). I returned to the academy for another six weeks of training. The same driving and pumping skills were taught, with the addition of ladder and Self-Contained Breathing Apparatus (SCBA) manipulative testing. The academic side of the academy wasn't an issue. The very se-

rious topic of wildland firefighter safety and survival was covered just before the final test day to drive home the point that we needed to be good students of fire behavior our entire career.

My very first assignment was at the Reedley station, part of the Mid-Valley Fire Protection District, covering behind another FAE that had been promoted to Fire Captain for the summer. I had ample opportunity to learn how to use the HURST tool, better known as the Jaws of Life, because there were many vehicle accidents to respond to.

One day we were fully staffed on our shift. The engine only had three seats up front. For the first and only time in my career, I had the opportunity to ride the tailboard. I felt at home with the wind in my face, and my smile was impossible to wipe away for the rest of the shift.

A few months later my time at Reedley ended, and I was transferred to Tranquility, an aptly named community in the heart of Fresno County's agricultural lands. I discovered that I still had much to learn about fighting fires, emergency medicine, and working with volunteer firefighters.

A two-person engine company does not have the luxury of specialization that larger companies provide. Both people get to vacuum the barracks floor. Both take turns scrubbing the toilet, and both people have to be in the thick of each and every call. Whatever lack of confidence I had when I first arrived in that battalion was pounded out of me by the time I left three years later.

For such a rural area, we had more than our fair share of high-speed car crashes to respond to. The HURST tool was perhaps the most used piece of equipment we carried on our engine. One time it took us nearly an hour to extricate a tow-truck driver who had fallen asleep and plowed into the backend of a semi-truck. Miraculously he survived, suffering only a broken ankle and clavicle. The farm worker, riding his bike home at night, was hit not once, but twice by hit-and-run drivers. He probably lost his leg; there just was no structural integrity to even attempt a traction splint. The human body is not designed for collisions much above 50 mph. It's just not.

Medical emergencies in rural areas also demand a toll. An 18-month old child was taking a nap while Mom worked in the kitchen. When she went to check on him, he wasn't breathing. By the time we arrived, the local clinic doctor was already doing compressions. The doctor glared at us when I explained we weren't paramedics. We took over CPR for the next several minutes, waiting for the medics to arrive. You do everything you can, because the family is there. When the flight nurse and the paramedics can't even tap a vein, you know what the outcome is, but you keep doing compressions anyhow until the child is loaded into the helicopter for their fruitless flight to the city.

Another CPR call on a woman who was not much older than I am now. We would get her back, and then she crashed again. We repeated that cycle for another twenty minutes before the hospital doctor finally called it. Even with the paramedics pushing IV fluids, she had lost too much blood to sustain life. Between us and the medic unit, someone had to stay on scene until the coroner arrived. We left and brought back the medics a couple of cold sodas. We arrived just in time for family members to start arriving at the house and verbally lash out at the only thing they could, the people who couldn't save their mother.

Then there was the early morning vehicle fire in the middle of nowhere, a car wrapped around a snapped off power pole. It's uncanny how a vehicle can leave a road and fail to find the gap between two poles a hundred feet apart. An elderly gentleman was walking around the wreckage as it burned. As my firefighter extinguished the car, I asked the man if he knew who the car belonged to. "My son", he said.

By then the sun was up enough and I could see that no one was ejected from the vehicle. I walked up to my firefighter and told him to be cognizant of the issue as he continued towards the driver's compartment. When the crusty veteran sergeant from the Sheriff's Office arrived, he asked why I had requested him for a vehicle fire.

I explained the situation and pointed towards the father. "I don't know what to say to him", just as the father picked up a tennis shoe next to the vehicle, and just as quickly dropped it.

After we extracted the victim so the coroners could take him, they stopped and looked at that shoe. One of the coroners picked it up and looked inside. He unzipped the body bag part way and dropped the shoe inside.

A vehicle full of teenagers and young adults overturned. Victims were scattered everywhere. One person was trapped underneath the vehicle, while passers-by kept the vehicle from rocking over any more than it already had. All that was visible was a pair of legs. Whomever it was, they were face-down in the sand of the roadside shoulder.

Dropping down to my knees, I could see the person's torso. I took my helmet off and crawled in as far as I could. "Hey, can you hear me?!" I shouted. To my surprise, she responded.

"What's your name?" I asked.

"Linda" she replied. Hmmm. Wasn't expecting that.

"Great name! My name is Linda too."

"Are you hurt anywhere? Can you crawl out?" No and no were her answers.

Assuring her that she would be okay, but that I had to leave to get some equipment, I left her side and hustled over to the engine to get some cribbing. As I tossed it off the top of the engine where we stored it, other firefighters grabbed the blocks to stabilize the vehicle. Next, I pulled the Hurst tool with the spreader attachment. Within moments the vehicle was lifted enough, and she crawled out on her own, uninjured. Just 14 years old, she had tagged along with an older sibling for a night out with the "in" crowd.

By the time I tested for Captain, I was ready for a change. I wanted to get back to the wildland side of the department, and the fastest way to do that in the late 1980s was to go into the fire camp program. By 1990, the right opportunity opened up and I left Fresno for the unit I had first met as an LT-FAE.

The Lake-Napa Unit, as it was known back then, was to be my home for the remainder of my career; another twenty-six years full of challenges, opportunities, sorrow, and growth.

Delta, the first time

Another reason I went into the camp program was to sharpen my skills in supervision. I believed that if I could motivate, train, and organize a firefighting crew staffed entirely by inmates, then I could supervise anyone.

As with all human beings, the old saying rings true, "They don't care what you know, unless they know you care." Also, there is a difference between delegated authority and respect due to position, and that which is earned one day at a time. I was taught by the senior captains to be fair, firm, and consistent. Not always the easiest personalities to work with, sometimes the inmates taught me.

Within six months, I was assigned my own crew. Other than time off for vacations or illnesses, I would be the primary captain for that crew for the next three years. By then I had established a reputation for my fairness, making it an easier transition.

I still had to spend time explaining my philosophy on work ethic, demonstrating advanced skills for firefighting, and setting boundaries for behavior when working in public areas where civilians might be. Inmates were rotated on a fairly regular basis, and I think by the time I left the camp, I had supervised well over a hundred different people on my crew.

I still consider my time at Delta as a Fire Captain one of the highlights of my career.

The East Side

Although the Administrative Captain position at the camp was being waved in front of me, I told the Chief that if one of the fire stations closer to my residence had an opening for a Captain, I was

going to go. My husband and I had started to drift apart, and I didn't want that to happen.

The major reason I felt it necessary to leave the camp program had a lot to do with a conversation my husband and I had one night. At the time he was working for a county-level juvenile detention facility. We had not seen each other for a couple of days, and when we got home for dinner that night the first few minutes of the conversation centered on who had had the worst "bad boy, bad boy, whatchya' gonna' do?" situation of the week. This was not a one-time discussion. It had happened way too much recently. Not healthy.

I worked for a statewide organization. I could work anywhere. So, when the Leesville station in Colusa County had an opening for a Captain, I jumped at it. One day I was covering a crew. The next day I was opening up the station for fire season.

Three nights later I received a phone call at the station from my sister Diane. Our brother Scot was dead. He had taken ill on a camping trip, and while his attendant left his side to go summon help, Scot aspirated on his own vomit. A week later we held a memorial service for him on the banks of the Sacramento River. I wondered why his roommate, a young man with Down's syndrome, could cry so easily for Scot, and I couldn't. I wouldn't know the answer to that question for another twenty-two years.

Lake County

After six years working in the East Side of the unit, rotating between assignments at each of the three stations in that battalion, I decided it was time for greener pastures. I had learned everything I was going to learn by working at one-engine stations. I needed to move to a two-engine station. I landed at the Kelsey-Cobb (KC) Station in Lake County. Other than moving my office five feet when I was later promoted to Battalion Chief, I would remain at that station for a dozen years.

Kelsey-Cobb is situated almost in the middle of the county.

Surrounded by large oak trees, during the summer it could be ten degrees cooler there than anywhere else in the county. During the winter an occasional dusting of snow enhanced the natural beauty of the landscape. I fell in love with the place.

During the summer fire season, the place had its own rhythm marked by the requirements of the job, punctuated by the pace of incidents both local and "out of county".

The two-engine station was busier than the one-engine stations just from a personnel perspective. With two fire captains, three fire apparatus engineers, and seven firefighters spread out over the week, on any given day there were 6-8 people at the station. A year later the Battalion Chief moved his office there, so some days there were more.

Our calls were not just limited to wildland fires. Due to the higher population density, we routinely responded to structure fires and vehicle accidents with the local fire agencies. Professional relationships grew into friendships as the years went by.

One summer we had the best group of firefighters I ever had the pleasure of working with. All of them were promoted to permanent assignments within a few years. Most are now fire captains working at stations, running camp crews, dispatching in the Emergency Command Center, or POST-certified law enforcement officers. It was a special group.

At the end of that season, a year-end gathering was planned in Tahoe. I don't normally attend these events, but this was a special group so both me and my partner Pat Ward attended. At one point we walked by one of those Wild West photo stores. What the heck, we decided, and we went in and "gussied up" for the picture.

Battalion Chief

In 2007 I was promoted to Battalion Chief in the same battalion I had been working as a Fire Captain. That created a few wrinkles with who had been my former peers, but we all survived that first

summer working together.

One of my first fires as a BC occurred in the Upper Lake area. A late afternoon start, it was being pushed by the normal late afternoon wind. The two hand crews that responded had already been on another fire earlier in the day and responded from there.

As the afternoon wore on and things got under control, one of the crew captains got on the tac net and made a pithy comment about lunch. "Boy, it sure would be nice to have a sack lunch!" His partner running the other crew acknowledged his comment with his own sarcastic remark.

I understood their sentiment. Working two fires in one day burns a lot of energy, especially for hand crews cutting line. Part of me wanted to release the first crew, but the inmates got paid by the hour on the fireline, and I didn't want to punish them for their captain's challenging behavior. The captain also could have just walked the crew back to the bus and passed out their rations. He had options, which included not openly challenging me that way.

I took the high road. I got on the same tac frequency and called my two division supervisors. Once they confirmed they were listening, I made the following announcement:

"Division A, Division Z, be advised I ordered sack lunches two hours ago. They will get here when they get here. I'll advise when they arrive."

There might have been a touch of acid added to the second sentence, but no one got on the radio to complain about being hungry again. The local government Fire Chief standing next to me nodded his head. "Nice play Linda, nice play."

Part of the job of the Incident Commander, which was my role on that fire, was to handle the logistics for the incident. When I made that phone call to the ECC two hours earlier, I organized and ordered a lot of things: sufficient personnel for night shift, fresh personnel for the next day's shift, Gatorade and drinking water, and lunches.

Early one morning we were dispatched to a vehicle crash with fire. The car had plowed into a tree at a high rate of speed. The people in the car he had just recklessly passed moments earlier came across the scene first, before the car had caught on fire. While the wife called 9-1-1, the husband (a retired CHP officer) tried to pull the man out. As the car started to burn, he kept trying to extract the driver, only abandoning his attempts when his own life started to be threatened by the encroaching flames.

A critical incident stress debriefing (CISD) was set up for within the next few days. One of the very few multi-agency CISD's I attended during my career, even the retired CHP officer was invited.

At sunrise though, we were dispatched to a structure fire in the Spring Valley area east of Clearlake Oaks. I was supposed to go off duty that morning, but until the other BC was ready to take coverage the call was mine to handle. As I turned into the driveway of the house, the nameplate for the address caught my attention. One of our retired dozer operators lived there. The house was fully engulfed by flames. The wife of the operator was at the scene and explained they had both exited the building, but he had gone back in to rescue their dog. He never came out.

The scene wasn't safe enough for the coroner's assistants to enter the rubble, so we had to extract him. I didn't want the engine crew that had already extracted one burn victim that morning to handle this process. I went in with the other engine crew to help lift him. After we placed him in the bag, we draped his body with a US flag in deference to his prior military service.

One evening the South Lake County FD paramedics from the Hidden Valley Lake station were dispatched mutual aid to a serious vehicle accident just south of Lower Lake. The highway had been totally closed, and the Fire Chief for Lake County FD (LCFD) had ordered multiple air ambulances. I responded to the call to help with the landing zone (LZ) for the helicopters.

Sure enough, once I was in the area, that was my assignment, so I posted up at the designated LZ and waited for the first helicopter

to arrive. My phone rang, it was the Chief. He advised me that the first patient being transported to the LZ was one of my off-duty fire captains. The ambulance arrived just about the same time as the air ambulance. I checked in on him, and as he was drifting in and out of consciousness, I left the medics to tend to him. I still had two more patients to coordinate flights for, a husband and wife. Unfortunately, they had to be sent to two separate trauma hospitals in two separate counties.

After the last of the helicopters took off, my phone rang again. It was the Chief again. "Can you come on up to the accident scene?", he requested. I drove the half mile to the scene. He greeted me at the front of my truck. I could see additional victims ahead, laying on the roadway - lifeless.

The Chief explained that the other three had been passengers in the fire captain's car, and the Highway Patrol was wondering if I could help identify them. I walked over and kneeled down to look at them. I recognized two of them but was unsure about the third person. They all looked very peaceful. I walked back to my truck and made a phone call to the Duty Chief. A CISD was being set up by LCFD. Once that was done, I wanted to go to the hospital, which would involve getting another BC to cover. It made for a very long night.

Back to Delta

I still had a goal to accomplish in my career. I wanted to be promoted to Assistant Chief, especially at a camp. Early in my captain days, I had identified that as one of my career goals. I spent some time in 2012 interviewing for various positions in the north state but came up short. Still, I used them as learning tools - and studied more in the areas that I needed to boost and waited for the next round of openings to occur.

Early in 2013, the right opportunity popped up on the radar. There was an opening at the camp where I used to be captain – Delta Conservation Camp. Several people told me I didn't have a chance, that another well-respected Battalion Chief was a strong candidate. I was stronger, and I knew it.

I discussed it with my husband. I had just reached the minimum age to retire. I could keep doing what I was doing as a BC, I could be. promoted, or I could retire. I didn't feel ready to retire yet. I was still enjoying the job too much. If I got the job, I would work through the 2016 fire season for retirement formula reasons too lengthy to discuss here. I would also have to commute and probably stay the night closer to the camp a couple nights a week. At 2:20 hrs. one way, it was just a bit far to make it a daily drive. With his concurrence, I applied for the job.

I showed up for my interview, spit polished in my Class A uniform. My heart was light - and I joked with the office staff. Once in the interview room, though, I turned on my "incident" intensity - and answered the questions thoroughly. Even the one that was improper to ask: "Given the recent health challenges of your husband, do you think it wise to take this job?"

"Wow," I thought. My husband had had a series of health challenges over the previous three years so I could understand where the concern was coming from, but it still caused me to pause for a second before answering, "Do you think I would be sitting here if I hadn't already discussed this at length with him? Do you think I would have even applied for the job if he had a serious ongoing health concern?"

My sources told me it wasn't even close. Still, it made for an interesting phone call from the Deputy Chief that would offer me the job a few days later. The only reason I bring it up is because it eventually plays out as a factor with my post-traumatic stress injury. After I accepted the job, the Chief continued and spoke without thinking, "I don't know if you're lying or not about being a team player..." I pulled away from the phone and looked at it. Did I just hear that right? For a split second I thought about telling him to "shove the *#$% job where the sun don't shine", but I thought better of it. A year later, after I signed my final probation report, we had a discussion about it and came to an understanding.

It wasn't until I moved to Headquarters a year and a half later to take the reins of the newly formed Central Division, that I learned that that particular chief had a habit of talking out of the side of his mouth when things didn't work out in his favor.

The Fire

The summer of 2015 started early and gave warning signs that it was going to be a bitch of a season. The Sky Fire burned aggressively for an early-season fire and created headaches for the firefighters due to the constant flow of spot fires. Only an assertive air attack kept it from growing to an extended or major fire category.

The Wragg Fire a few weeks later made the Sky Fire look tame by comparison. Within an hour it was impacting a popular hiking trail. And yes, there happened to be a couple of friends at the top of the ridge covered with brush taller than they were. The Helitack crew rescued them with minutes to spare. Another woman, who had gone out for a peaceful run on the trail, ran the race of her life along the lower half of the trail to get back to the roadway and safety.

The Rocky Fire started in a remote area of Lake County. Fires that start in that area typically burn a hundred or so acres by the time they are contained. Within an hour I could see the header from the Emergency Command Center in St. Helena. It was 8,000 acres by nightfall and would not be contained for days.

Just as that fire was wrapping up, another one started. I had finally gotten a day off and was at the local brewpub O'Meara's having dinner and a pint of chocolate stout with my family. I could see the header through the window and realized my time off would be cut short. The Jerusalem Fire thankfully was burning in an unpopulated portion of Lake County. Other than a wind shift that pushed the fire towards the Hidden Valley Lakes subdivision for a while, creating some tension, this fire was just fatiguing because it had started on the heels of the Rocky Fire.

Another couple of smaller fires followed. By then the unit was humming along at a high frequency of efficiency. On most of the previous fires I had functioned as the Unit Duty Chief. Timing is everything, right? Jokingly, I started referring to myself as the "shit magnet".

The Peterson Fire was different though. I happened to be in the Lakeport area when this fire started in the hills above the Highland Springs reservoir. Due to the potential threat to structures on the east side of the fire, I responded there, already knowing the on-duty Battalion Chief Greg Bertelli had responded to the west side of the fire. As I helped the local chiefs get their engines deployed, I finally had a chance to observe the early fire behavior first-hand. I was watching a crown fire run downhill through the 100 ft tall pines. Observable probability of ignition was at least 90%. It was impressive to watch, and it greatly enhanced my understanding of the fire behavior that had been experienced on the other fires that summer.

The Air Attack Group Supervisor (ATGS) requested the use of VLAT's (very large air tankers). Specifically, he wanted to get the MAFFS (Modular Airborne Fire Fighting Systems) from McClellan. He assured me they were still available, and with their 3,000 gallon payload, they could quickly build a box of retardant ahead of the fire and keep it from running through the lighter fuel towards a more densely populated area of the county.

I approved their use, the tactic worked, and by nightfall we had a shaky containment line built around the fire. A few more days of mop-up and patrol put that one to bed.

Early September blessed us with another fire on the southern boundary of the Mendocino National Forest along Elk Mountain Road. Yes, I was the Unit Duty Chief again. The local Division Chief was on jury duty, so I was assigned as the Agency Representative for the fire and headed that way. By nightfall, we had the fire relatively boxed in below the ridge, and I believed we would be handing the fire off to the Forest in the morning for ongoing management of the incident. However, the USFS requested that we manage the fire because they were heavily tapped out due to multiple lightning-caused fires further north in the state.

My role turned to Incident Commander, and I spent the next several days assigned to the fire. A heat wave hit mid-week - and with temperatures well above 100 degrees for several days, we were collectively relieved that the heatwave had not happened a few days earlier. The Elk Fire, you see, was the first fire that summer that had behaved relatively normal for a Lake County fire.

By Friday, I had signed the last of multiple financial documents related to the incident and headed home for a weekend off for the first time in nearly a month. It was also September 11th, and I always take a moment to remember the thousands of souls lost in 2001 on that fateful day.

Section 2

Unknowing:
The Calm Before
The Storm Of Discovery
2015

The Valley Fire
My Fire

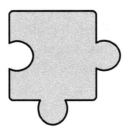

BEFORE

Friday, September 11, 2015 marked the 14th anniversary of the terrorist attacks in New York City, Washington DC and Pennsylvania. There's not a First Responder in this country that can't tell you where and what they were doing on that day in 2001.

I was in the El Dorado National Forest, working as a Line Safety Officer on the Starr Fire. We had just finished our morning operational briefing and I was picking up my sack lunch, when the vendor asked if I was going to be packing my gun that day. I thought he had mistaken me for a security guard, because I had not yet donned my yellow Nomex. When he repeated the question, I jokingly asked if bears had been in the food area, a very real concern in that part of the forest.

He cocked his head, looking extremely serious and responded, "You don't know, do ya'?"

The towers had yet to collapse at that point in time, although that was only moments away. The rest of that story, as Paul Harvey would say, is history. I bring this up because firefighters mark the path through their careers by such memorable calls.

For many of us that work in northern California, we would soon have another such memorable day.

The state of California is prone to wildland fires during the summer. Multiple local, state and federal agencies have various levels of responsibility to deal with them. The agency I worked for, the California Department of Forestry & Fire Protection (CAL FIRE) provides wildland fire protection to over 31 million acres of land from San Diego County in the south end of the state, up to Siskiyou County in the north. The department is broken up into twenty-one administrative units, to provide better management to deal with issues at the local level.

I worked for the Sonoma-Lake-Napa Unit (LNU), just north of the San Francisco Bay Area. The unit is large, covering land from the Pacific Ocean inland some 80 miles east to the Interstate 5 corridor, and from Interstate 80 northward to the Mendocino National Forest, located north of Clear Lake. If there is vegetation that is prone to burn during the summer, it lives here: grass, brush, timber; we have it all. It can be cool and foggy near the ocean and be 105°F in some of the inland valleys. The terrain varies from relatively flat land, used primarily for agricultural and urban purposes, to steep inaccessible country. The unit burns well and has had its share of large damaging fires over the years.

The 2014 fire season in California was ugly. Several large wildland fires occurred throughout the state, many exhibiting extreme fire behavior. Firefighters were seriously injured. The community of Weed in Siskiyou County had the wind-driven Boles Fire push through town, destroying several homes in the process.

The winter of 2014/15 was dry, adding to a fourth year of drought in the state. The drought added its own element of stress to the landscape - as bone-dry fuel burns really well, and opened the door for a bark-beetle infestation in timber covered lands, killing millions of trees over thousands of acres.

All of this had fire officials worried entering the 2015 fire season.

CAL FIRE ramped up its staffing for the summer, hiring its seasonal workforce earlier than normal.

Locally, the Sky Fire got the ball rolling on July 6, 2015 in the foothills north of Vacaville. Although it started relatively early in the day, the fire confounded efforts to control it. Access for fire engines was fairly easy, and considering the fire was burning in grass, it should have been easy to control. The fire had other plans though, and kept throwing out embers, which started new fires as they landed in the dry grass. These spot fires kept the crews busy for a while, until a strong aerial attack with air tankers dropping retardant on the hillside finally brought the fire into check at 150 acres.

The Elk Fire had behaved relatively well, compared to other fires in recent weeks. With the shorter days of September ahead, firefighters were hoping that the corner had been turned for the year. Barring a *foehn wind* event later in the fall, everyone was somewhat hopeful that things would return to "normal" for the remainder of the fire season.

By the time September 12, 2015 rolled around, the unit had already had six significant fires. The fact that the historical "peak" fire season was just beginning, generated some concern. How to best manage fatigue that a long fire season can manifest was being discussed at the highest levels of the department

SEPTEMBER 12

During the morning of September 12, CAL FIRE Battalion Chief Greg Bertelli attended a Fire Safe Council meeting in Middletown. "Bert", as he was known to friends, left the meeting just after noon - and noticed a west wind blowing. "Not a good day for a fire," he thought. After having lunch with the Middletown station personnel, he drove up Highway 175 to Cobb, and then turned onto Bottlerock Road. Bert continued to drive north towards Kelseyville, hoping to tie in with a group of new volunteers during their training to staff Konocti Lookout in the future.

Although there was a Region staffing pattern to hold personnel on duty to support the Butte Fire in the Amador/Calaveras county area, I stayed at home that morning. I had worked through the previous weekend on the Elk Fire and had a few chores to catch up on. In particular, I wanted to start repairing the common fence with our neighbor. His wife had been very ill recently, and his Anatolian Shepherd dog had nearly escaped the previous week. It was overcast - and only in the 80's that day, but I had put on a long-sleeved shirt because I didn't want to get sunburned.

As I finished up a late lunch, I noticed my work phone was flashing a blue light, indicating a CAD page had come in. A new fire had been reported in the Cobb area. I knew Bert was on duty, and my friend and partner Jim Wright lived close by. Still, I grabbed my Cobra scanner as I went out to work on the fence.

IGNITION

It takes only *one* spark to start a fire; that – a receptive fuel bed – and some clean air. All three were readily available at 1:20 pm on September 12, 2015. Within moments of that *one* spark – the fire was noticed by a neighbor, and they quickly called 9-1-1 to report the fire across the street from their house on High Valley Road, near the community of Cobb. The concern in their voice was noticeable. The fire was already a half acre in size and – as the caller described the scene to the dispatcher – it started to burn towards another house. Shouting could be heard in the background, as other neighbors grabbed garden hoses in an attempt to stop the fire. By the time the person reporting the fire got off the phone, the fire was estimated to be three acres in size.

Each administrative unit for CAL FIRE has an Emergency Command Center (ECC). For Sonoma-Lake-Napa, that ECC is located just north of St. Helena in Napa County. During the afternoon, it is usually staffed with two Fire Captains and two Communication Operators. Once they receive a report of a new emergency, they enter the address and call type into the Computer-Aided Dispatch

(CAD) program. CAD quickly identifies where the closest available resources are. While that is going on, someone else gets on the radio and gives a "pre-alert" with the basic call type, the general location, and the nearest station.

When St. Helena announced "Vegetation Fire, High Valley Road, Kelsey-Cobb" everyone working in Lake County that day knew they would be going.

Within two minutes of receiving the 9-1-1 call, St. Helena ECC dispatched the initial attack resources: one battalion chief, six fire engines, two transports with dozers, one water tender, one hand crew, an air attack ship, two air tankers and a helicopter. Other than the number of hand crews, this is the standard attack for a vegetation fire on a HIGH dispatch day. That's not to say that all of these units were the normal line-up for the area. Due to the Butte Fire in Amador County, several fire crews were not in the county. LNU had utilized their assistance-by-hire policy to backfill behind the missing equipment. When the "pre-alert" tones sounded, personnel stopped what they were doing, and prepared to respond.

St. Helena rattled off the dispatch information: "B1418, AA140, T85, T86, C104, E1491, E1487, E6031, E1495, E1464, E6221, M6311, T14E1, T1443, WT6411, KON1, crew to be announced, vegetation fire, 8015 High Valley Road, Valley IC, LNU East, VFIRE22." LNU East, one of the primary dispatch frequencies for the unit, was designated as the COMMAND frequency, while VFIRE22 was identified as the TACTICAL frequency.

The crew of Engine 1495 was in Kelseyville, providing training to the Konocti Lookout volunteers. They apologized for having to leave before the training was complete.

The crew from Copter 104 walked out to the helipad and looked north for the smoke. The reported location was fairly close to the base. They debated whether to drive to the fire due to the potential problem of finding a suitable landing zone near the fire, but finally decided to fly in.

BC Bertelli had just driven past High Valley Road on his way to Kelseyville. He didn't recall seeing any smoke as he drove by. He turned around near Harrington Flat Road. As he headed south again on Bottlerock Road, he could finally see the column from a vantage point near the Moore Family Winery. His initial report to St. Helena was that there was a good column visible with a west wind on it, and he requested an additional helicopter and air tanker. Bert also made the request that Chief Wright, the Operations Chief for the North Division, be notified of the new fire.

A few moments later Joe Baldwin, the newly appointed LNU Fire Prevention Bureau Battalion Chief, announced he was responding to the fire. As a fire captain for several years, Baldwin had supervised inmate fire crews, been a station captain at Clearlake Oaks, and most recently had worked as one of the fire captains assigned to the Boggs Mountain Helitack Base in Cobb. Used to fighting fires from the head – or leading edge – of a fire, he was still getting used to his new role: respond to the origin to determine the cause.

As the pilot of C104 completed his pre-flight check and spooled up the helicopter, the crew put on their Personal Protective Equipment (PPE). Each crew member had their assigned role. One fire captain sat in the front next to the pilot, while the other captain took a seat in the back with the firefighters. The pilot, Tom Humann, was a former Marine Corps pilot, and had earned a seat as one of the pilots for Marine One, the presidential helicopter. Pat Ward was the senior captain, with nearly ten years' experience as a Helitack captain. The other captain, Warren Parrish, was in his 4th year working at the Helitack base. All of the firefighters were experienced, no rookies allowed. The firefighters had spent time on engines and had been recommended to the Helitack base by their captains.

The role of a Helitack crew is to provide a quick attack, holding a fire in check while ground based resources gain access and start a more systematic attack. Helitack crews use hand tools such as pulaskis and McLeods, back pumps, and chainsaws. They are fast and mobile, and coupled with support from their helicopter making bucket drops of water, usually darn effective. About ten minutes after the Valley Fire started, C104 was circling overhead, getting the

first real look at what the fire was doing. Pat Ward's report on conditions indicated the fire was two acres in size, burning in grassy oak woodland, with a moderate rate of spread, and one structure was currently threatened. He estimated it had the potential to go about twenty acres and requested that everyone on the dispatch keep responding.

By then B1418 had made access to the fire, driving in on High Valley Road. He agreed with the initial size-up provided by C104, but the west wind was a real concern. Bert noticed other structures in the area as well. Based on his assessment, he ordered two more dozers, hand crews, water tenders, and five more fire engines.

After BC Bertelli drove through the fire area on High Valley Road, he returned to Bottlerock Road because that was the general direction the fire was heading towards. Recognizing the need to evacuate people early on, his initial action was to evacuate the residences west of Bottlerock Road, due to their close proximity to the fire's path. It would also make it easier to provide structure defense without the civilian population getting in the way.

Air Attack 140, responding from the air attack base at the Charles Schultz Airport just north of Santa Rosa, requested three additional multi-engine air tankers. Unlike the Rocky and Jerusalem Fires earlier in the summer, the Valley Fire started in a more populated area. It was shaping up to be a long afternoon.

As Bert was getting his resources lined out, the ECC was busy answering 9-1-1 calls. A caller from Bottlerock Road said the fire didn't appear to be too big, but he saw black smoke earlier, and asked if anyone was at the scene yet. The black smoke undoubtedly was from the first structure that burned during the fire. That caller was also the first to ask if there were any evacuation orders yet. Another caller from High Valley Road asked if he should leave considering the guys from the helicopter were right there.

A third caller actually thought CAL FIRE was doing a control burn. "At this time of year? Wow!" After it was explained that it was a *real* fire, he responded "Oh, I thought you guys were burning..."

Additional 9-1-1 calls came into the ECC. More and more people could see the growing column of smoke. Several reported that ash was falling into their yard. The main question that seemed to be on most callers' minds was "Do I need to evacuate?" They were told that no order to evacuate had been given, but if they felt threatened – they should leave the area.

As I walked outside to dig holes for new fence posts, I was listening to the scanner. I heard Bert direct the first due engine to respond to the threatened structure on High Valley Road, and then request another chief officer if Chief Wright wasn't available. St. Helena told Bert that Wright had an extended ETA and they would find another chief officer.

Never being one to miss a good firefight, I walked back inside and grabbed my phone. Chris Veilluex, one of the fire captains working in the ECC that day, answered my call. Still listening to the scanner, I asked about Jim's status, and was told that Jim was out of the immediate area but was responding. I told Chris I would respond.

I quickly changed into my work clothes and called out to my husband Curtis as I walked out the front door: "New fire in Cobb, see you later tonight sometime".

While St. Helena toned out more stations to respond to the fire, I put on my PPE. Normally I'd just put on my Nomex shirt until I got into the area of the fire. Given the worn-out state of my right knee, my hands-on firefighting days were well behind me, so I rarely strayed far from the beaten path. Somehow though, that just didn't seem like the right thing to do that day, so I put on *all* of my Nomex before driving away from my house. I also drove Code 3 through the residential neighborhood I live in, another rarity for me. I usually save that for when I get to Highway 29, only a half mile away from my home.

While I was still driving through town, I heard Bert give his operational objective, to keep the fire west of Bottlerock Road. He also made a request to evacuate High Valley Road and along Bottlerock Road. I acknowledged my response with St. Helena and let them

know I was aware of the evacuation order. Even driving Code 3, it would take me twenty-five minutes to get into the fire area.

As I passed Kelseyville, Bertelli expanded the evacuation area to include the length of Bottlerock Road. As the fire continued to escalate in intensity, and spotted across Bottlerock Road, Bertelli adjusted his evacuation order to include all of Cobb.

Meanwhile, the Command Center went about their business of filling all of the orders that had been placed by the Air Attack and the Incident Commander. The Mendocino Unit agreed to send a hand crew strike team, and a bulldozer. The Northern Operation Center, in Redding, called for an update on the fire. North Ops (NOPS) provides coordination between the different CAL FIRE units in the northern part of California, along with the various National Forests. The United States Forest Service (USFS) was overloaded already with a series of lightning fires in the far northern part of the state, and CAL FIRE already had a significant response to the Butte Fire over in the central Sierras. Firefighting resources were stretched a bit thin.

"What is the fire doing?" NOPS asked.

Chris Veillux calmly responded, "The initial report was three acres, with a moderate rate of spread, and multiple structures threatened. We have committed everything, our crews, all four dozers."

"Okay, Santa Clara Unit will provide a strike of engines to cover behind, and you know NOPS doesn't have much. If you need more dozers, go the hired route."

At the end of the call, the NOPS Duty Chief told the captain in the ECC, "Good luck."

MAYDAY

"Good luck."

Have you ever watched a football game, and heard the announcer state that the quarterback hasn't thrown an interception in his last 200 pass attempts? If you follow the game at all, you know the quarterback has just been jinxed. Not only will he throw one interception, but he will throw two more for good measure, or fumble the ball on a crucial drive late in the game. As a sports fan, I wince when an announcer does that.

So, had I been on the phone that afternoon with the NOPS chief – and he told me that "The region has limited equipment to support your fire", and "What can you kick loose by the way?" – I would have cringed at the comment, "Good Luck". Thanks for your support.

As I turned onto Bottlerock Road, I requested a road closure for Bottlerock from Highway 29 all the way to Cobb, and also for Highway 175 in the Cobb area. I'll be honest – given that it was Saturday; I didn't want a bunch of "looky-loo's" plugging up the roadway. With on-going evacuations, our law enforcement partners didn't need that added pressure either.

Meanwhile, the St. Helena Emergency Command Center (SHECC) was fielding multiple calls on their 9-1-1 lines. A few callers lived on Fox Drive and could see the smoke column from their houses. Although the fire was still primarily west of Bottlerock Road, they were told to evacuate based on the most current report from the Incident Commander. Other callers – in much closer proximity to the fire – were requesting direct assistance at their residences. With the first few engines already at the scene committed to fighting the fire, Bertelli had to respond to one of the requests himself, as there was no one else immediately available.

I was still driving south on Bottlerock Road towards the fire. The northern end of Bottlerock Road meanders through rolling hills covered with California chaparral, and is lightly populated. As the road continues up the face of the Long Ridge, the vegetation transitions to manzanita and timber. More people live up here, shaded from the hot summer sun. Harrington Flat Road intersects with Bottlerock Road here, and heads off through the forest towards the east. Just south of this intersection is a local landmark, the Snake Ranch, which is where Bertelli was when the fire was reported. Just another

quarter mile to a turnoff into Calpine, usually locked up as it is rarely used.

Once I was past the Calpine gate, I knew I would finally be able to see the smoke column. For a brief time, Bottlerock Road leaves the forest, as it makes a sharp left turn before dropping down into the High Valley area. From that bend in the road, I was able to clearly see the column. It was white, and dense from top to bottom. The base of the column was hidden behind a small ridge. The top end was truncated, like a tulip, but it didn't appear to have a significant wind on it otherwise.

The afternoon winds in Lake County had tended to appear about 2 o'clock, so I wasn't too surprised by the truncated top. The sky was covered with a high layer of mammatus clouds, well above the top of Cobb Mountain at 4,721 feet. I briefly debated whether the fire had enough energy to break through the cloud layer. There was a significant gap between the tip of the smoke column, and the cloud base. Based on what I was saw, I didn't think much of the odds. I contacted Bertelli on the radio, and we agreed to meet at his command post located at Bottlerock Road and High Valley Road, just a few minutes away. As I dropped down the hill, I lost sight of the smoke.

Before I arrived at our meeting location, the ECC reported that a disabled resident needed help evacuating from their home on Bottlerock. I scribbled the address on my hand while I was driving and started to look for it. Bertelli acknowledged the radio traffic, and reported that he would handle it, as all other resources were already committed. As I drove by the Yogi Bear RV Park, I thought it would make a great place to stage equipment.

Still looking for the address, I continued south past High Valley Road. There was no drift smoke, flames or anything else that would appear to be amiss or indicate the presence of a nearby fire. I finally saw Bertelli heading north around a bend in the road and pulled over by a driveway. I glanced at the address post and realized I had driven past the address in question.

Bertelli pulled over and walked up to my passenger window. Knowing that time was an issue, I asked for a brief update on the fire, along with a sketch of the fire area. I was going to take Command of the incident, and have Bert take the role of Operations. It was beneficial to have both people working from the same game plan, and I needed that to get him the assistance he needed to fight the fire.

St. Helena tried to contact me on the radio, but I wanted to be finished with the transition meeting as soon as possible, so I told them to stand by.

As Bert quickly drew a map for me, I sensed something was a bit off. I've known Bert for years and fought a lot of fire with him. When he flipped the map at me, I knew something was amiss. "What's going on, Bert?

He finally spit out, "Did you hear the Mayday traffic?"

Mayday traffic?! Stunned by the words, I quietly responded "No, no I did not hear that. Fill me in." Bert quickly explained that the crew of C104 had been burned over.

"All of the crew?"

"No, not all of them. I think they are in shelters."

Okay, got that.

I gave Bert one very clear direction, "Go find them!"

With that, he got back in his truck and drove off. As he did so, I reached for the radio microphone to call the Command Center. Not everything has to be reported promptly. If the fire had slopped over the containment line, that's relatively normal, and I would have waited a few minutes to report it. A burn-over situation, however, is not normal and there was no way in hell I was going to sit on that information.

"St. Helena-D1409…Priority Traffic…still working on transition with 1418, I'll be taking the IC…Be advised there has been a shelter deployment for the crew of C104, hold non-essential (radio) traffic only until we switch over to a command frequency."

I have no idea what happened in the Command Center when they received the message. I never asked, but I could tell from listening to the radio and phone recordings from that time period that their stress level spiked.

One of the Comm Ops got on the air, and calmly asked if there was a need for an air ambulance or a medic unit. Not knowing the answer to that underlying question, I requested one medic to respond to the nearby fire station in Cobb. Almost immediately, Valley Air Attack overrode my call. BC Chris Jurasek was in the air that day, and without hesitation ordered up two ground medics and two air ambulances. The intensity in his voice left me no doubt that he knew the full story of the burn over.

That conversation brought me back to the immediate needs of the incident. Knowing the fire had been reported east of Bottlerock, I told St. Helena that power lines were down, and to make a Life Safety Alert to all incoming resources. I didn't know at that particular moment in time if any lines were down or not, but considering the totality of the circumstances, I felt certain they would soon be, if not already.

I still hadn't seen any drift smoke across Bottlerock Road, but I needed to know where the fire had spotted across. Due to the circumstances around our transition meeting, I had to get my own information, so I put my truck in gear, and headed south again. Just after I rounded the next bend in the road, I found the smoke - heavy white smoke, driven across the road by a brisk wind. Embers as large as horse flies surfed the current at eye level. I decided to continue on until I cleared the drift smoke, then I could stop and get my bearings. As I drove, I could see a few spot fires in the meadow east of the road, but not the main fire.

I proceeded south on Bottlerock Road while listening to the radio traffic concerning the crew's situation. As I continued to drive through the heavy smoke, I could see even more spot fires east of the road. The moment of silence was broken by another call from the ECC. "Just confirming that you would like the entire community of Cobb evacuated?"

Still mulling over the initial impact from the news of the Mayday, I couldn't recall if I had heard that request from Bertelli over the radio. At that time, I just had to trust Bert. If he ordered it, it needed to be done. Before I even cleared the drift smoke, I replied back to the ECC. "Affirmative…need to evacuate Cobb."

I was actually surprised, and concerned about how far I traveled before getting back into clean air. I drove a good half mile before I finally stopped. Forced to look over my right shoulder first because of a new muscle spasm in my neck, I realized I was parked in front of a friend's house. The fire was coming down the hill behind his house, partially sheltered from the wind. A neighbor was trying to beat out a 20-foot wide spot fire in the front pasture.

I had to turn my shoulders to look left, and liked that view even less. The meadow was full of spot fires. I contacted St. Helena again to provide an updated report on conditions, confirming that the fire had crossed Bottlerock Road and added – with a touch of anxiety – that there were more spot fires than I could count. I also told them I was taking the Incident Command at that time. On scene for less than ten minutes, **somewhere – deep in my brain – I felt a heavy door slam shut.**

What I know now about how the brain functions under duress, that "door" slamming shut was my brain doing its best to compartmentalize the stress that it deemed to be overwhelming. In this case, it was the news of the burn-over. The term for this attempt at self-protection is dissociation.

It wasn't until I tried to hail a nearby water tender did I realize that I didn't have the correct tactical frequency on my command group scan list. I quickly deleted the frequencies used during the Elk Fire earlier that week and dialed up the correct frequency. I could then hear the radio traffic between the crew of C104 and Division Chief Jim Wright. Jim knew the area like the back of his hand. I recognized the voice of the captain, Pat Ward, as he stated their approximate location. Between Jim and Bert, I knew the rescue effort was in good hands. I turned my attention back to the fire.

With multiple spot fires east of Bottlerock Road, I knew we needed more resources. Valley Air Attack was already building an air force with additional air tankers and helicopters on order coming from throughout the north state. Fortunately, even with all of the recent fire activity there were plenty available. I thought for a few minutes on what to order for the ground attack.

Lake County had a few challenges due to its terrain. Surrounded by mountains, reinforcements took some time getting into the area. CAL FIRE had six engines stationed in the county. If more were needed, they traveled in from Colusa, Napa or Mendocino counties. Fortunately, the local fire districts had a well-rehearsed drill for activating a county task force of engines. Even though they had not yet been requested, I felt fairly certain they were already being organized, because I know the Fire Chiefs around the county. The sketch Bert gave to me showed five engines already at the scene, and I knew more were on their way to cover the empty stations around the county. I had also heard Bert order more water tenders; a routine request due to the limited water supply in the area.

Anything I ordered would take time to arrive. There is a reflex time associated with a large order for equipment, related to the process itself. If I ordered CAL FIRE engines, St. Helena would fill what they could from within the unit and send any additional needs to North OPS. From there, NOPS would split up the order and send requests to other units that they already knew had equipment to spare. The bigger the request, the greater distance the equipment would be responding from. All of this went through my brain in a fraction of second. I placed a big order anyhow.

I already had a mental image of where the "big box" of the fire might end up. The north side would go from Bottlerock over to the Ettawa Spring area, while the south side would go towards Harbin Hot Springs. The far side of the box would be Big Canyon Road. If the fire got across Highway 175, there weren't many other options.

While I was writing out my order, St. Helena contacted me to conduct a radio test for a new Command frequency. I told them to hold off on that because I wanted them to start processing my order first. One of the things I learned as a young fire captain was to go big or go home. I was fortunate to have learned from chiefs such as Tom Tarp, Ron Childress and Ed Stadelhofer. They were aggressive with their fire attacks, and not afraid to go all in. Without hesitation, I went all in. My order was for three Branch Directors and eight Division Supervisors. I would need them to coordinate the ground attack, along with BC Bertelli. I also ordered forty Type 3 fire engines. I wanted the closest available, and I wanted them Code 3 to the fire. In addition, I wanted twenty hand crews, ten bulldozers and ten water tenders. All of that, I wanted "immediate need" to the fire.

"Immediate need" assignments differ from "move up and cover" assignments. The primary difference is the sense of urgency. An "immediate need" request is asking for the closest available resource, regardless of agency ownership, to arrive as soon as possible. It allows for the difference between Code 3 driving with lights and siren, and Code 2 driving which is drive quickly, but otherwise obey all traffic laws.

It was already about 2:25 in the afternoon. I hoped to have some of that equipment inside of an hour, knowing deep in my heart that it would be two hours or more.

As I finished placing my order on the radio, I looked up just in time to see Jim's truck drive by. Sitting on the tool boxes in the back were a group of firefighters, wrapped in fire shelters. "Okay", I thought, "they're safe. I can check that box off my list. They're safe."

I turned my truck around to watch the fire behavior for a bit. None of the spot fires were really taking off. There just wasn't any equipment available to jump on them. I decided to take a "Zen" moment and clear my mind. I needed the clarity that a moment of meditation would provide. I'm not sure how long I sat there, but when a dozer transport set its air brakes just outside the cab of my pick-up, I knew it was time to move. FC John Jensen walked up to my window and said he was going to take action with the dozer, first to protect Jim's place, then to work towards Cobb. I told him to do the best he could and turned around again to drive into Cobb.

I heard Unit Chief 1400, Scott Upton, hail me on the radio. He wanted me to place a phone call to him. Although I had decent cell coverage where I was, I knew he wanted information I didn't have yet; an update on the conditions of the Boggs firefighters. I stalled and told him I would call when I had better reception. I headed up to Boggs to find out what I could.

BOGGS

I didn't find out until days later how the injured firefighters got up to the helibase. I just knew that was where I would find them. The helitack base is routinely used by REACH as a landing zone in the area, so it seemed highly probable they had been transported up the hill in the back of D1403's truck. I was wrong about that particular point.

C104 landed at the intersection of Bottlerock Road and Sawmill Flat Road. The injured firefighters were quickly assessed for injuries and given some cool water to drink. The extreme heat they had endured had sapped them of all strength. They were then assisted into the helicopter and flown up to the helitack base for additional treatment while waiting for paramedics to arrive.

I pulled into the parking lot by the office and backed in. From my vantage point, I could see a firefighter sitting on a wooden box at the edge of the grassy helipad. His Nomex shirt looked charred on the shoulder. I frowned. It takes exposure to several hundred degrees to char Nomex like that. As I walked up to the helipad, FC Warren Parrish came out of the helicopter hangar with an armload of cold bottled water. He asked me to grab more water out of the fridge inside. I did as he asked and followed him over to the injured firefighter I had seen earlier.

As I walked, the scene seemed surreal. One of the injured firefighters walked by me already talking to someone on his cell phone. "Zombie" was my initial thought. "He looks like a zombie." I looked over to my right. Another of the injured FF's was on the ground, writhing in pain while another firefighter comforted him, and I noted that an IV had been started. That's when I realized REACH was already on the ground, parked behind C-104.

The injured firefighter I had initially observed sitting on the box turned out to be Pat Ward. As I scanned him over during a visual head to toe assessment, I recognized that his injuries were very serious. His hands were burned significantly, and I wondered if he would ever be able to ever play bagpipes again.

As I kneeled down to unload the water bottles, Pat acknowledged my presence. He looked absolutely exhausted. Surprisingly so, considering his extreme fitness level. "I'd ask how you're doing, Pat, but I can see for myself…" *Pretty fucked up* was left unspoken.

The flight nurse from REACH approached, stating that Pat had the worse injuries of the four of them. I stood up to talk with him, reminding the nurse that CAL FIRE's policy for burn injuries required transportation to the nearest burn center for assessment and ongoing treatment. He assured me that knew the policy well and they would all get taken to the UC Davis Burn Center in Sacramento.

As I pivoted away from Pat to allow the nurse the space to work, I stumbled, feeling what? Spaced out? No, that would be the polite way to describe what I was feeling. **"Horrified" would be the correct word, although it would be 18 months before I could say that word out loud.** Even though Pat and I argued over many things, I still liked him. **Part of me was ready to bolt and get the hell out of there.** Mercifully, the feeling only lasted a couple of seconds. As I walked back towards the office, I picked up my cell phone, which I had dropped while carrying the water. I still owed the chief a phone call.

I strode into the office and reached for the landline. I didn't want to rely on a cell signal for this particular call. Once I had Upton on the phone, I quickly described the nature of the injuries I had observed, and who was involved. After that short discussion surrounding Serious Accident Review Team (SART) activations, Upton focused back on the fire.

"What do you think, do we need a team?" Ordering an incident

management team is a significant investment, and the decision is not taken lightly. We had already had three team deployments in our unit that summer, two of them in Lake County for the Rocky and the Jerusalem Fires. At that time, the Valley Fire had not yet made its first hard run up the hill. Knowing that more fire engines were on their way in to the area, I asked for time.

"Give me two hours," I asked, "or if it crosses 175, then order the team." I figured I had one shot, and – even with a lot of aggressive firefighting – it was going to be close. Upton agreed with my request, told me he had a few phone calls to make, and then he would be up in the area soon. With that, we ended our call.

I got back in my pick-up to leave the base, still partially wanting to stay and help with the injured crew. An ambulance from Lake County FD pulled into the driveway right then and, with the medical attention the crew needed well in play, I started to drive out of the forest. Before I got to Highway 175, the second ambulance arrived, from Lakeport FD. Recognizing the paramedic on board, Eric Lund, I stopped to give a short briefing.

"There are four burned firefighters up there. Take good care of them."

After his initial shock wore off, he acknowledged with "You got it, chief!" I thanked them and drove to the stop sign at 175. As I turned north on the highway, I swore there would <u>not</u> be a thousand more burn injuries that day, not on my watch, and **another door slammed shut in my brain.**

It still seemed much longer, but the elapsed time from when I announced the shelter deployment to getting back on Highway 175 was only thirty-two minutes. However, a lot can happen in half an hour and I knew I needed to see what the fire was doing. I had to get my eyes on the smoke column again. The fastest way to do that was to get near the golf course, where I could clearly see the sky. I advised St. Helena that I was going to get a quick look at the fire, and then I would head over to the South Lake County FPD station in Cobb to establish my Command Post.

I headed north on 175 towards Harrington Flat Road. Before I got there, I dropped down onto Snead Drive and started looking over my shoulder to catch a glimpse of the column. With too many houses and trees in the way, coupled with my persistent muscle spasm, I circled around the north end of the Adams Springs Golf Course to Lema Drive. Once I got south of Lema Court, I finally had a clear view of the column, and I did not like what I saw at all. The column was still white, so the fire was still burning in vegetation, but the base had spread about another 25-30%. Even worse, the entire column had tilted over about 30 degrees. I really don't recall what four-letter word spilled out of my mouth, but it seemed highly appropriate at the time. The last thing I needed that afternoon was a wind-driven fire. **I actually winced in physical pain as my brain found a third door to slam shut**, and my window of opportunity kept shrinking.

As I reflect back on that moment, for several months I thought that this "door" thing was future-oriented. It wasn't though. Being advised of the burn-over was, in its own way, a blindside. My initial view of the smoke column did not correlate to a dangerous fire. My initial view of the rescued firefighters, as they were shuttled past me in the back of Jim's truck, did not equate to the injuries I eventually witnessed. The enormity of the situation, at this particular moment, just couldn't be consciously acknowledged. There wasn't time for it. **My brain did the best it could to put the past behind me, slamming doors as it went about its business of saving me from myself.**

HOBERGS

The Valley Fire posed several problems that day. The initial problem of just fighting the fire was challenging enough. Rescuing our own firefighters during the first hour added to the complexity. Environmental factors, including drought conditions and that unanticipated wind event, turned this fire into a Type I incident at the blink of an eye. Evacuating people off a mountain with a limited number of law enforcement officers, people's own notion of how they should be notified before leaving, and a road system that would soon be compromised by the fire itself, required split-second decisions.

I hustled back up Emerford Drive to Highway 175 and turned back towards Cobb. As I drove by the Hobergs Resort, I saw Lakeport Fire Chief 500 Doug Hutchison parked alongside the road. He was in charge of the county task force of engines, so I knew at least a few more engines would be in the area soon. As he approached the area, Chief 500 contacted me on the radio, asking for some direction on where to deploy his engines. I told him to come in on Highway 175 and start towards the Estate Road area, because initially that's where I thought the fire would go. I wasn't so sure now. I drove by him, because I noticed when I first drove by the resort that there were guests there. I pulled in, and an employee approached my truck.

I stated, "You need to get your guests out of here." In retrospect, I can see it from his perspective. All he had to go on was my word. There was no smoke in the area, no flames, no fire engines, no air tankers dropping retardant, no helicopters circling overhead. Other than two chiefs in pick-ups with their Code 3 lights on, there was no real evidence that anything was amiss.

"Are we in imminent danger?" he responded calmly. I was too busy playing sports in high school to bother with the debate club, but even I still realized that I needed to pause before answering his question. I recognized that the word *imminent* had various shades of definition, but it just wasn't the time to come to a common understanding of the word, so I changed tack, and told him the current state of affairs.

"Look, there's a vegetation fire on this side of Bottlerock, I already have four burned firefighters, and the fire has a wind on it. I don't know if I can stop it before it gets here. You need to leave." Once he started to nod his head with understanding, I trusted he would do the right thing, so I left to continue on my way to the Command Post.

Before I got there, though, I wanted to see what was happening down by the Pine Summit Pool. I dropped down Summit Boulevard to Hobergs Drive. I saw a couple of engines at the edge of homes along Trinity Road. I hadn't really been in the area since I was promoted to Division Chief in 2013, but I spent quite some time driving around previously both as a fire captain and as a battalion chief. That had been my initial attack area for a dozen years. Instead of continuing along Hobergs back towards Emerford Road, I continued up the hill. Within moments I came to a dead-end. I had forgotten that Hobergs ended there.

At the end of the cul-de-sac was the Sugar Pine Pre-School. A small one-story home converted to a pre-school, it was tucked underneath a shady grove of pine. Outdoor play equipment was in the side yard along the road's edge. Once I got over my irritation at driving up a dead-end road, I thought about the school.

"It's Saturday – and no one's here. That's good, I don't have to worry about evacuating them." Then the revelation hit me like a ton of bricks. If they're not here, then they're at home, somewhere *around* here. And they're in danger. **An immediate sense of dread spread over me. I felt extremely claustrophobic and I remember thinking at the time "That's weird, because I 'm not claustrophobic."** My brain had other ideas though. The wind-driven fire was somewhere behind and below me, and I was at a dead-end. **Once again, my brain slammed shut a heavy metal gate with an iron-clad clang.** That was the final one.

Before that, I had never ever experienced claustrophobia. Over the years, I have crawled under unstable cars to calm trapped peo-

ple. When I worked in the Mid-Valley Fire Protection District in Fresno County, my captain, Dennis Green, routinely sent me up into the attic at house fires. He was 6′2″, I was only 5′ 7″. Guess who got to crawl into tight spaces? I've even maneuvered my way through fire pump plumbing to get a wrench on a gate valve that needed repair, which was really funny when we got dispatched to a call just as I reached over to loosen the damn bolt.

That afternoon though, was no laughing matter, and I quickly turned around. As I started to work my way back out, I stopped my truck and reached over to grab the microphone for the PA system. **Time slowed down to a crawl as my brain kept asking my hands what they were doing as they adjusted the volume.** The hands never responded, they just kept fiddling with the knobs on the Unitrol. After a couple test clicks on the transmit button, and another final volume adjustment, I returned to real time and started to drive through the neighborhood telling people to evacuate. I back-tracked my route until I got to Glenn Road where I turned right and continued my announcements.

Intentionally using a calm tone of voice I announced, "Evacuate. Please evacuate. You need to evacuate. Now." I didn't want people to panic, myself included. I chirped my air horn every now and then to get people's attention. I saw people coming out onto their porches, so I thought I was having some success getting the message out there.

As I circled down around onto Shasta, I saw two men in the street talking. I stopped and rolled down my passenger window and told them they needed to evacuate.

"Yeah, we know", one of them replied, and went back to his conversation. I saw a woman loading stuff into the trunk of her car, with no apparent sense of urgency. This was frustrating for me. They *know* we've already had two major fires in this county this summer that required rapid evacuations so why are they moving at a vacation pace? Again, there was no smoke in the area so all I could do was keep on driving and making evacuation announcements.

When I got back to Summit Boulevard, I looked down the hill towards the two engines I had seen earlier. I was about to drive down to their location when St. Helena announced a new fire at Gifford Springs Road. "Really? You've got to be kidding me!", I thought as I kept making evacuation announcements. I drove back up to Highway 175, past Humboldt Drive, then responded to the new fire.

ESCALATION

Even after listening to the recordings, I'm still not sure what happened first. Regardless, at approximately 2:55 pm the Valley Fire cleared its throat and roared to life. In a span of ninety seconds, multiple 9-1-1 calls were made to report the fire at Highway 175 and Gifford Springs Road, the helitack base requested three additional air ambulances to transport the injured firefighters, and Valley Air Attack reported the fire was across (east of) Bottlerock Road, approximately 200 acres in size, burning through grass, oak and timber.

The Air Attack also added that the fire had "spotted up towards Hobergs Loop, Bluess Court...moderate to rapid rate of spread with multiple long-range spotting."

As Valley Air Attack circled over the Gifford Springs area, he reported the "fire going down the hill towards Middletown, burning in the flats, structures threatened, one acre in size".

In the midst of all this, St. Helena was still receiving 9-1-1 calls for emergencies not related to the fire. We were still using the East frequency as our Command net, while they still needed it to dispatch new calls. It seemed like everyone was trying to talk on the frequency at the same time. As the repeater got overworked, sound started to degrade and there was a lot of garbled radio traffic.

Fighting fire in the wildland-urban interface (WUI) is complicated. It's also extremely dangerous. California fire history is full of stories of burned over crews along with burned up fire engines. Earlier in the decade FIRESCOPE finally adopted formal WUI guidelines. It ensured a common language, common tactics, and key operational

parameters. It was also in alignment with the key priorities for CAL FIRE: protect life, property and natural resources, in that order.

Finally, Bertelli was able to get ahold of me on the radio to discuss operational priorities. Based on his observation of the fire's behavior – making an uphill run in alignment with the wind – safety was at the top of the list.

In less than a minute we identified our Leader's Intent: Evacuation of the civilian population, Prep & Go tactics, and situational awareness of the first responders for their own escape routes and safety zones. We also determined that switching over to our newly assigned Command frequency wouldn't be possible right then due to the dynamic evacuation situation in the Cobb area. St. Helena would just have to wait on that.

Tension grew as the fire got closer to Boggs Forest. The injured firefighters were still receiving initial treatment at the helipad. Valley Air Attack contacted the helitack base to advise that the fire was right below their location. This coincides with a 9-1-1 report of a house on fire on Summit Boulevard.

Meanwhile, St. Helena was still waiting for a break in the radio traffic to dispatch personnel and equipment to the fire near Gifford Springs. Once I confirmed that they knew about the new fire, I cleared the air for them. St. Helena told me they had two reports of a fire at Gifford Springs and Highway 175, and another fire just south of that intersection. I had just driven up Gifford Springs Road a quarter mile or so, and had only seen the one fire burning in the meadow. Still, I reminded St. Helena that we were already stretched pretty thin, and anything they could send would be appreciated.

Battalion Chief 1410, Paul Fleckenstein, arrived in the area and provided an update on the fire, "At least four to five structures immediately threatened..." With another battalion chief to share the load, I left the Gifford Springs fire in his capable hands. Meanwhile, Valley Air Attack provided an unpleasant update on the fire's spread.

"St. Helena, Valley Air Attack with an update…fire has made it through Hobergs, across Highway 175, and is now established in Boggs Mountain State Forest. Moderate to rapid rate of spread, 400 acres of timber."

I didn't think St. Helena heard the update initially, because Valley Air Attack had to repeat it. I heard it though and realized that I had a different type of monster to deal with. It took ninety minutes for the fire to get to 200 acres. It doubled in size in just seven minutes. With visions of the Peterson Fire quickly turning into a crown fire as it burned through timber, the Valley Fire had just turned the corner from an extended attack fire into a major fire.

As the fire encroached upon the Boggs Helitack Base, the two firefighters most seriously injured were loaded up on REACH 6 and REACH 18 for transportation to the burn center at UC DAVIS Hospital in Sacramento.

At 3:13 pm Valley Air Attack made contact with the base and tersely told them "You need to expedite."

The two remaining injured firefighters were loaded onto C-104, along with the Paramedic from Lake County FPD, for the 45-minute flight to the hospital. The remaining people at the helitack base turned their attention to their own situation and started to prep the structures for defense against the flame front.

Further up in the forest, Prevention 1422 and B1420 Joe Baldwin were finishing a quick sweep of the forest. Two empty campsites had been found; the occupants unaccounted for. By 3:25 pm Baldwin reported the fire was at the access road, burning fast to the base, becoming inaccessible. Both officers retreated to the base and assisted with its protection.

Four burned firefighters, an on-going evacuation, and two separate fires. Just two hours into the incident, and I had a bloody mess on my hands. I pulled into the front parking area at Station 62, the initial location of my Command Post.

I started to press on some critical safety issues. I reminded St. Helena to advise all incoming resources of downed power lines as they

entered the area. Wooden power poles would be easily damaged in a fire of that intensity; the cross-arms wouldn't stand a chance.

I also asked for an update on their ability to acquire additional tactical frequencies. When several fires are burning in the state, frequencies become a hot commodity. That day was no different. A frequency allocation group is tasked with assigning frequencies so that they don't interfere, not only between fires, but also for normal local usage. More fires equal fewer options. Still, I needed more frequencies *badly!* I informed St. Helena that we had overwhelmed the few we had, and that it was priority for safety. Two minutes later they called me back with three additional tactical frequencies, along with the two we were already using. Glad to have anything, I quickly relayed the information to Operations.

In the realm of the Incident Command System, there are eight key functions equally split between Command and General Staff. Within the General Staff are the Finance Section Chief, the Logistics Section Chief, the Operations Section Chief, and the Planning Section Chief. For the Command Staff, there is the Incident Commander, a Safety Officer, a Liaison Officer, and an Information Officer. If a position is unfilled, it falls to the next highest person within the organization to take care of those responsibilities.

I already had my Operations Chief, with Greg Bertelli filling that role. The other three General Staff positions were not high on my list of concerns right then. Although I had served as the Incident Safety Officer on an Incident Management Team (IMT #1: First to Serve) for CAL FIRE, I needed to pass that to someone, so I ordered three Safety Officers for the fire. I also knew that this fire was going to draw a significant amount of media attention, so I ordered two PIO's to respond to the incident.

I grabbed my portable radio and got out of my truck. I needed to move. I walked inside the station for a quick restroom break, noting that the power was out. Just after I returned to my truck a service technician from PG&E walked up and inquired what I needed.

"I need you to turn off all the power on this mountain."

"All of it?" he questioned, as he raised an eyebrow.

"Remember that snow storm we had a few years back? You did it then. This fire is going to destroy power poles all over the place. I don't want firefighters or civilians to get hurt because of that."

He took off. I never saw him again that night. But I heard that he, and a handful of his partners, put themselves into harm's way to kill the power on the mountain. Everything had to be done manually, and they were in the middle of it for the next several hours.

The sound of the first explosion drifted my direction, carried by the wind. Then another explosion. Then another, even louder. After a couple minutes of this I looked at the clock in my truck, taking a mental note of the time. As the explosions continued, some louder than others, I mumbled under my breath, "My boys are getting their butts handed to them."

I had known many of them for several years. I knew them as new firefighters. I knew them as they moved up to Fire Apparatus Engineer, onwards to Fire Captain, and in Bert's case, to Battalion Chief. They were friends, and they were family. And I was worried for their safety. Deeply worried.

Prevention 1426, Fire Captain Dave Munch, advised St. Helena that he was responding from the Highway 20 area. Dave had been on his way to the Butte Fire when he heard the fire traffic. He stopped in Williams and contacted the ECC. After a few phone calls, he got himself relieved from that response and was returning to Lake County.

Battalion Chief Paul Duncan called me on the phone and assured me that he was available to respond. His wife had just had back surgery the day before, but I could use the help, so I told him to come on up. He responded from his home in Hidden Valley Lake.

In the midst of all this activity, explosions could be heard from my location. At first, it was just a random pop or two. I attributed them to smaller propane tanks used for barbeques. No doubt they

would BLEVE (boiling liquid expanding vapor explosion) when exposed to the fire front. I tried to contact Bert on the radio with no success. As time went on, there were even more explosions. The Sheriff's Office relayed via radio that the 6000-gallon propane tank at Hoberg's Resort was threatened by the fire.

My mind drifted to thoughts of my son-in-law Kevin. During his 22-year career with the Marines, he had seen his share of action overseas. I wondered if this cascade of explosions was similar to what he had experienced. I caught myself then and chided myself for even trying to make the comparison. Even if this is what a mortar attack sounds like, *this* will be over in a couple hours, not continue on for months on end.

As I continued to call Bert on the radio, hoping to get together to discuss strategy, the explosions changed in frequency and intensity. The engine crews last seen on Trinity Road had taken shelter with civilians at the Pine Summit Pool as the fire exploded around them. They would eventually report that not only were the propane tanks exploding, but so were the trees.

I had been trying to reach Bert for over twenty minutes as these explosions were occurring. My initial thought was that he was busy with evacuations. As the minutes ticked by, **I started to get angry. When he failed to answer again, I threw my microphone off the dashboard,** just as Paul Fleckenstein walked up to my truck. He understood my frustration, as we discussed what was going on with his fire. I advised him that due to the close proximity and limited air space, his fire would be absorbed into the Valley Fire as its own branch. The plan was to do that when we switched to the new Command frequency.

After he walked back to his truck, still feeling slightly embarrassed at losing my cool like that in front of someone, I reminded myself that calm is contagious and vowed to cork the negativity for the rest of the day. Taking a deep breath, I refocused on the problem at hand – Bert wasn't answering his radio, and I was worried for his personal safety.

Fire Captain Doyle Head showed up in his personal vehicle. He needed to get up to Boggs to get his gear so he could assist. He was on vacation, but when he heard about the helicopter crew, his wife basically kicked him out of the house and told him to get to work. Doyle tried to drive up 175 but returned within minutes. The fire was actively burning across 175, and it was too dangerous to continue.

He asked if there was a utility vehicle somewhere, and I told him there was one by the forester's office. He tried again to go up the hill and returned. I told him to wait another ten to fifteen minutes, to let things cool down a bit. Doyle was a person of action, and I knew he was frustrated. Finally, he took off up the hill and I didn't see him again for several minutes. When he returned, he had all of his gear, and the utility pick-up. He told me the helitack base was still standing, but the rest of Cobb didn't look so hot. Actually, that part of Cobb was very hot. By the time I drove through the area two days later, only a single house was left standing.

By then I had heard from Bert, and I directed him to report to the Command Post. We had work to do. Upton arrived just then and told me Assistant Chief Todd Derum was enroute to take over Operations. Upton left to go observe the fire personally. A few minutes later Bert pulled in next to me, and slumped over in his seat, looking totally exhausted. He had been in the thick of it trying to get people to evacuate. I had about three seconds to figure out how to tell him he was being replaced by Todd as the Operations Chief on the fire and – considering how he looked – to do it in such a way as to not question his abilities. I was glad when he protested, and I assured him I needed him in the fight, because I did.

After Todd arrived at the Command Post, and they had a few minutes to discuss strategy, I advised them we had to move the Command Post to Middletown and that, with the initial critical evacuations handled, we had to switch our Command frequency.

With our law enforcement representative in tow, we started to drive down Highway 175. The Gifford Springs Fire, by then dubbed the Valley 2 Fire, had jumped the highway near Arroyo Vista Road.

Burning debris was scattered along the highway, reminding me of one evening on the McNally Fire in Kern County in 2002, where a crown fire had closed down an access road. Eventually, though, we cleared that fire area and proceeded down the highway. The view of the ridgeline to the north of us was obliterated by heavy dense smoke. The fire was rolling along, consuming everything in its path.

With each bend in the road, I expected to catch up with the head of the fire, but that didn't happen. I watched as the near horizontal smoke column rolled in on itself. "Plume dominated fire behavior?", I thought to myself. By the time we got to the Dry Creek Cutoff, I quit watching the smoke. I had nearly rear-ended the pickup ahead of me and had yet to catch up with the head of the fire.

I received confirmation from Prevention 1426 that Harbin Hot Springs had been evacuated just as the fire was bearing down on it. The fire growth was explosive, with spot fires being reported by the Valley Air Attack a mile ahead of the main fire. One arm of the fire was making a beeline for Middletown, the other was approaching the southern end of Hidden Valley Lakes. Valley Air Attack doubted if they'd be able to continue flying air tankers much longer due to the wind speed and turbulence. Their primary mission had been to protect the evacuation routes up to that point.

MORNING

As the night faded away to morning, the next phase of the firefight was just ramping up. The morning operational briefing was to be held at the Konocti Conservation Camp, a minimum security CDCR facility jointly operated with CAL FIRE. The inmates were used to staff five firefighting crews, with fire captains from CAL FIRE leading them. The camp had been used countless times over the years as a base and staging area for wildland fires in Lake County. Given the fire activity in the county that summer, it was set up to support crews since the beginning of the Rocky Fire in late July. It wouldn't totally return to normal operations until mid-October.

Unit Chief Scott Upton stopped by the Middletown command post on his way to Konocti. I hadn't seen him for a few hours and asked him how he was doing. He had gone back to his office at St. Helena Headquarters to make several phone calls relating to the fire and to the injured firefighters. Sometime in the middle of the night he had had a chance to grab a short catnap in his office. I'm sure the carpeted floor was comfortable, but it was no substitute for a real bed. Still, I know from experience that beggars can't be choosers, and even an hour of shut-eye is a powerful thing.

He reminded me that I needed to be at the briefing. I checked my phone and figured I would need to leave about 45 minutes before the briefing, to allow time to work around downed lines, and whatever else was blocking the road by then. Highway 29 was blocked by several downed power lines on the bridge over the St. Helena Creek. A Prius might have been able to squeeze under them, but not a pickup truck with a light bar. Some of the personnel that were en route to the camp from the Middletown area could be heard on the radio talking about four-wheeling across the creek.

Finally, a little after six, I left the Command Post to start driving north. A few people were following me to help get through the road blocks, including Pam Perdue from PG&E. I already knew the apartments had caught fire, but I was still surprised to see how much damage they had incurred. Just a couple blocks down from the station I looked north up Berry Street. One of our retired Heavy Fire Equipment Operators, Ken Leuzinger, lived just up the block off Highway 175. I didn't see his house or garage and felt sad about that.

We got to the bridge, and it was obvious we weren't going that way. The sun had come up enough so I could look up and down the creek a ways. I got out of my truck to see if I could figure out where everyone else had crossed over, but then noticed that not everyone with me had a 4WD vehicle. I would have to find another way. I noticed some traffic on St. Helena Creek Road and saw where they had crossed over. I had forgotten about the old bridge on Wardlaw Street. We turned around and turned behind Store 24. As the sun

continued to rise, the destruction became more obvious.

We headed north on Highway 29, but before we got to the Bar-X Ranch we found our way blocked by a low-hanging phone line. A service truck was moving into position to attempt to move it. Pam Perdue had advised me of the phone line earlier that morning. They weren't sure if they could just cut it, the concern being it might be the main trunk line into the Middletown area. That was also the same line that had prevented the fuel truck from making it into town earlier that day. Where there's a will, there's a way, and the PG&E crews figured it out fairly quickly. They wrapped a rope around the line and lifted it up with a boom truck. I'm not sure what they did for the remainder of the day, but for the moment the highway was clear for us to proceed north.

As we approached the field where Crazy Creek Glider Port was located, another disturbing sight came into view. Abandoned cars were along the edge of the road, in both directions. Not just abandoned, but burned out hulls. One car was off the road down a bank. Both sides of the highway were burned bare. All I remember thinking at the time was "Where are they? Where are the people? Did they get out? Did someone pick them up?"

"Are they okay?" My hope wavered. Buildings can be re-built, but for the first time I was truly troubled about the potential loss of life. "Did we get everyone out in time?" For the first time that morning, I doubted it. "Did we, did I, just kill a hundred people?" That last thought haunted me for days.

As we continued north, aided by the rising sun, I could see further out to each side. Hidden Valley Auto Body was just a twisted metal sculpture of its former self. Havy's Restaurant was gone. Another burned car on the road. What I could see of Hidden Valley Lakes didn't look too bad, but the most damaged area east of Hartmann Road wasn't visible from the highway.

A mile or so north of Hidden Valley I saw a spot fire on the east side of the highway. The main fire was hung up on the hills to the west, backing down towards the highway. The last area I saw the fire was just south of Murphy's Springs Road. I could hear radio traffic on the tactical frequency as day shift resources were getting in place to catch that corner of the fire. They would bring the fire down to the highway and conduct a firing operation south towards Spruce Grove Road Extension.

We pulled into the camp, already late for the briefing. As I approached the briefing area, I was a bit disappointed by the size of the crowd. We normally had more people in attendance for a 1000-acre fire, but I also realized that some of the resources I had ordered several hours earlier were still inbound. The order for this morning had been massive. The state would have to dig deep to find what was needed, and some of it wasn't in the state.

After the briefing I met with Mike Parkes, our Deputy Chief of Operations. He would be the Incident Commander for the day, until the incoming Incident Management Team had completed their transition process later that afternoon. I introduced him to some of our cooperators, including the PG&E representative. It was a very informal cooperators meeting but getting their contact information and concerns was an important part of the process.

Afterwards, we had breakfast with Scott Upton. We were joined by Fire Captain Chris Vallerga Jr., assigned to Konocti Crew 5. They had been on the initial attack of the fire. He brought his crew in for a hot meal, but they would be going right back out to the line. I have known the Vallerga family for years; I had worked with Chris Sr. for many years prior to his retirement from the department.

I walked with Chris back towards the parking area. He was tired and cranky, and he needed to vent. Over the course of the night, he and his crew were chased out three different times by the fire. Anger and frustration were a common theme those first hours of the fire; his thoughts were no different.

Scott finally told me to go home and get some sleep. I hadn't been pulling hose or swinging a tool all night, so I wasn't physically exhausted, but I was absolutely mentally exhausted. I called home and let my husband know I was on the way, and no need for breakfast.

Twenty hours after I left the house, I pulled into the driveway. I got out of my truck and took off my Nomex. Only then did I realize I smelled like a structure fire, dirty ashtray, and chemical goop all rolled up into one noxious mess. A hot shower was my top priority.

Just as my head hit the pillow, my phone rang. It was Scott Drew, a retired division chief from our department. He asked about Ron Childress's home in Hidden Valley. Had it burned? I didn't think it had, and let Scott know that, and then I asked about Ron. Fortunately, Ron was out of the area and was fine. I assured Scott that I would make an inquiry and keep him posted. I called Parkes to pose the question. Mike was glad Ron was okay, and let me know that he had several employees, both retired and current, to track down to get their status. Other than the fire, that was one of his priorities for the day. I thanked him, and finally fell asleep.

Firefighter's Prayer

When I am called to duty, God,
wherever flames may rage,
give me strength to save a life,
whatever be its age.
Help me embrace a little child
before it is too late,
or save an older person from
the horror of that fate.
Enable me to be alert,
and hear the weakest shout,
quickly and efficiently
to put the fire out.
I want to fill my calling,
to give the best in me,
to guard my friend and neighbor,
and protect his property.
And if according to Your will
I must answer death's call,
bless with your protecting hand,
my family one and all

- Author Unknown

How Did I Get Here?
The Good, the Bad, and the Ugly

NOTE: These journal entries were written on the date noted so they are, in essence, my PTSD journey – in real time. Type in **BOLD PRINT** is a symptom of Post-Traumatic Stress, as it manifested in my life.

November 30, 2015

After visit with Doc

Wind: as a trigger

Recognize you are in a good place. And take comfort in that.

Listen to "wind" audio daily to help reset.

Take credit for the good outcome.

Remember previous calls with positive feedback.

Flip negative self-talk into a positive and ask, "What would I do next?"

SECTION 3

LOST IN THE WILDERNESS

2016

Discovery
An Inconvenient Truth

By the end of 2015, I was pretty desperate to break out of my rut. I felt caged, unable to get out of my own way. I had already seen my doctor to address my **insomnia**. After several weeks of getting enough sleep, thanks to pharmacological intervention, I felt ready to get back into my normal groove. Therapy was helping me see that things were not as gloomy as I thought, and to turn my focus towards rebuilding, towards reconstruction.

Buoyed by such support, I challenged myself to do something totally different, to learn something new, to challenge myself again. I tried to put a positive spin on every negative thought I had. My Facebook feed was intentionally front-loaded with positive vibes. I watched and listened to motivational videos on YouTube. I got outside of myself and went searching for the real me.

In January 2016, pretty sure that this was going to be the final year of my career I wanted to go out as strong as possible. Get things done. A fire or two, getting back in the saddle – so to speak – would help quite a bit with **my sense of self-worth.** Another reason I stayed for that summer – I didn't want the Valley Fire to be my <u>last</u> command.

I hired a life coach to help me elevate my performance towards the *high* range. In hindsight I can tell you this – it was the *best* thing I did in all of 2016. Here's why.

I learned enough about myself that spring, *reminded* myself of who I was and who I wanted to be moving forward. I essentially built new cairns along the path to my true self. Some cairns had already been built, knocked askew by the rough road of life, and just needed to be readjusted a bit. Others were new discoveries, such as being more creative than I had ever given myself credit for, and worthy of further exploration.

As spring turned to summer, though, **I sensed a growing confusion and felt increasing irritability return to my life.** The demands of the job required the cessation of my sleep medication. At first, I was able to sleep just fine. As the days turned into weeks though, **sleep became less restful and night terrors became an almost nightly occurrence. My "Incredible Hulk" persona returned,** especially after work.

Some days **I felt like Jekyll and Hyde.** Things could be going along quite well, without a hint of discontent, and then *bam!* The "negative" switch would be flipped to the ON position making it utterly impossible to return to a good mood in the same day. I was really off my game.

I hated going to the office and I would **create diversions** to avoid going there. What I know now, is that the two primary routes to the office both took me through the burn scar of the Valley Fire. I was being **triggered by the mile**, regardless of the route I took.

Finally, on July 5, 2016 I was **diagnosed with PTSD, with "delayed expression"** – a fancy term that meant it just took a while for the damn thing to fully come alive. At that particular moment, I actually felt a great sense of relief. **I wasn't going crazy.** There was a legitimate reason for all those feelings. [DSM-V, p. 274]

GATEWAY

I naively thought that just knowing what was wrong would somehow insulate me from the effects of my PTS injury. As much as I tried not to dwell on them, the symptoms were still there. Other than my husband and the therapist, I saw no reason to share the good news about my sanity. Except for one other person, no one outside of immediate family knew the troubled path I was on.

One thing the therapist questioned me about that day was my **apparent obsession with alcohol**. I think I was complaining about the skunky beer taking up space in my fridge. Or perhaps I was expressing my concern about a co-worker's excessive intake. Either way, she didn't so much as question me, as she did challenge me about my relationship with alcohol.

By the time I got home two hours later, I was **royally pissed off**. Just to prove her wrong, I poured out the beer (actually it was hard cider – still skunky though) and vowed to take a 90-day sabbatical from alcohol. If it was going to help with the healing process, then it was worth it.

As I laid in bed that night, **mad at the world, I finally admitted to myself that I was scared**. I didn't know enough about PTS to have even half a clue what I was up against. Whatever was taught at the Academy, and all subsequent training, didn't go in depth about the effects of PTS – not on you, the individual, let alone on your family that is forced to go along for the ride.

About midnight, I sent a text message out to an old friend. It had been probably two or three years since we last crossed paths. He had a couple of things going for him as my primary choice of reaching out for an understanding ear. First, he was retired. Second, and more importantly, he had already gone through his own recovery. I wasn't expecting an immediate response, but there it was just a few minutes later.

"How can I help?"

Four of the sweetest words a person can hear when they are in pain.

We texted back and forth for a bit and agreed to meet for coffee later in the week. My **anxiety** was calmed by the assurance of the meeting, and I was finally able to drift off to sleep.

ACCEPTANCE

A few days later we met for coffee. After exchanging pleasantries, I cut to the chase. Partly because I hate small talk, and partly because my **anxiety was ramping up**. "I have a bigger problem than alcohol", I explained. My friend raised his brow and waited. "I was just diagnosed with PTSD, and I was hoping you could help me understand it better. What am I up against?"

My friend didn't shy away from openly celebrating his years of sobriety. It was why I reached out to him to begin with. The rest of his story was not as well known, and at the risk of sharing his story without his permission, I'm not naming this good friend of mine here and I'm going to keep it short. You see, I knew he had been exposed to the demons of PTSD through his work. He helped a lot of people then. I was hoping he could help one more person – me.

One day in early September I was **feeling particularly pissed** about work, and I fired off a bunch of heated text messages to my friend. After this had gone on for a few minutes, he finally texted back, "Read page 417." I had just recently started to attend AA meetings, and was still getting acquainted with the "Big Book" of Alcoholics Anonymous. I thumbed to the recommended page and started reading.

Some things are out of my control. The politics of Estonia? Out of my control. The weather 100 miles away? Out of my control. What somebody says about me? Yeah, that's right. That's out of my control too. What I do control is what I *think* about those things. I control what I *believe* about those things. I control what *actions* I take in response to those things. Accepting something as the way it *is* doesn't mean I need to like it. Once I learned to accept something – such as my post-traumatic stress injury – I quit wasting energy on frivolous things.

I felt like a weight had been lifted from my shoulders. I realized I could keep fighting against my post-traumatic stress, like a wild mustang fights being trained for the saddle, or I could find a way within myself to accept it and instead expend that energy on getting better. The choice was mine. [Alcoholics Anonymous, p.417-19]

QUARTER 1: JANUARY - MARCH

NOTE: These journal entries were written on the date noted so they are, in essence, my PTSD journey – in real time.

Type in **BOLD PRINT** is a symptom of Post-Traumatic Stress, as it manifested in my life.

Saturday, January 8

Haven't journaled for a while.

Word for the day: **Irritating**

Diane is fixing the bathroom shower. Called in contractor. Wants to tile the shower stall, so today we drove over to Ukiah, picked up her friend Kim. Tile store went fast. Then we helped her with a linoleum issue. Then lunch. Anyhow, we were **gone for 5 fucking hours**. And I still needed to clear the carport. Curt and Mike had **done NOTHING** while we were gone, so we all pitched in. Backed in the truck and unbolted the shell. I asked Curt how we were going to lift the shell with what he had bought. Asked him to diagram it. Anyhow, what he bought wasn't going to work. To KMART to buy straps. We got the shell off. Won't be able to back all the way in with a load of pellets anymore. Can't drive forward into carport either.

Not sure what I really accomplished today, other than getting fucking mad.

Yesterday Diane and Curt both made somewhat snarky comments about my clothes in the front room.

I'm trying to get back to my happy place, but sometimes I just wonder.

Not sure I'm at the point where I can say
"What was, was" and let it go.

Sunday, January 9

Gratitude.

For my husband Curtis.

For his support on this crazy ride!

In a weird way, for the Valley Fire.

Drove me to face my old demons, and some new ones too.

And maybe back to my life purpose.

Helping others.

For my dogs.

They love me no matter what.

Live each day with Intention.

Friday, January 15

Blew up last night over a relatively minor issue. Stormed out of house. Walked to O'Meara's. Called Mike for a ride home. He called BS on me! Which I deserved.

Apologized this morning to Curtis. But I let Diane leave for work without doing the same. I think I need to meet her as she gets off work, 'cause she is going to Galt for the weekend.

Live your life with intention, Linda!

POSITIVE INTENTION!!

Bring the joy!

Idiot.

Wednesday, March 2

Hmm, have not journaled for a while. Mid-January?

Anyhow, we shall turn this into a gratitude journal. See how it goes...

HPA (High Performance Academy) last weekend in San Diego. Met a lot of interesting and caring people from all over the world.

And Peter, the Hero!

One person I met was Sparky (Helice Bridges)

She is a character!!

Watched her TED talk. Great idea.

I need to order some ribbons.

And send her a paragraph about the book.

Actually, had a decent conversation with the chief.

Long discussion with Lee Griffith about the HP (High Performance) coaching challenge. Pricey, but **I want to hit on all cylinders again!**

12 weeks one on one +

12 weeks small group

[Growth/HPI]

Had dinner with Mike at O'Meara's. Good times.

Thursday, March 3

Warm puppy at my feet

Great lunch – salad and some veggie stir-fry

Quit trying the computer

Brendon's videos play fine on the tablet.

Watched two parts of Thought Leader Road Map

[Burchard, TLRM, online]

Friday, March 4

Really got to focus on the Colusa Academy today.

Taught class tonight. Good group. Good energy. Jeremiah and Ben are doing good in their roles.

Had lunch with ECC staff. Funny!

People still got the HPAAAAAA spirit! (Brendon)

Oh, and **my favorite distraction** COC (Clash of Clans).

Hogs are now Level 5

[Clash of Clans, online video game]

Monday, March 7

Reviewed HPA notes. Made note cards INTENTIONS

Signed up for coaching

Interviewed for Unit Chief test.

Didn't totally suck.

Just lost my voice an hour before!

Breath work really helped.

Nice and calm entering interview.

Tile work done for fireplace.

Really nice job!

Made time to read a couple of articles on LinkedIn.

Wednesday, March 9

Oops – missed a day.

But grateful for the good night's sleep I had Tuesday night.

Our pellet stove is back in service!

Checked in with Shane Beck. He is doing well in Fresno County Fire

Sent Sparky an email with story info

Update on Pat Ward continues to be amazing

Friday, March 10

Lots, lots, lots of rain.

Starting to develop ideas for LT FAE refresher training. More hands-on, behind the wheel.

Really awesome soup for lunch today, made by the ECC staff.

Confirmation of radio interview about book this Sunday.

(not in the mood for gratitude on Friday. Long day)

Saturday, March 12

Went to the "office" today.

Turned on computer.

Transcribed phone calls to reconnect with the story.

Today is the six-month anniversary of the Valley Fire.

Discovered that Cheri Lynn, one of the students (in the academy) lives in Cobb.

Resilient!

Looking forward to radio show tomorrow.

10 days in a row, taking breaks.

Sunday, March 13

Had breakfast with Ken and Karen.

Always good for a laugh!

Had coffee with Kimberly.

Radio show today with Kimberly, Betsy Cawn, and Q.

Went well.

According to family, I did good.

[KPFZ FM 88.1, show]

Dogs are goofy!

I made sure I ate veggies with my dinner.

Still raining.

Very green outside. Very, very green. Most ponds and lakes have filled up. Clear Lake is FULL!

Monday, March 14

Saw Dr. Kopp today

I think I needed that.

Sunshine today! Getting a break from the rain.

Made progress on (Mom's) probate paperwork.

Started homework for 1st coaching session next week. Introductory questions. Yeah!

Curt made a very tasty chicken veggie soup for dinner with Hawaiian sea salt.

Tuesday, March 15

Thankful for my chiropractor!

And the help at the bank today with the estate account. Apparently, Willie has been talking about me!

Had lunch with Curtis at Main Street Café. Cruised over in the Sprint.

I need to drive it more!

Played with Schatze this morning until her tongue was hanging. Of course, she wanted more.

Checked out a CPA business. Well-established. Gives back to the community. Made appointment to handle Mom's estate and trust issues.

Wednesday, March 16

Had a good talk with Willie today.

It's been a while since we last talked.

Curtis set up the coffee for tomorrow. Even though he hates to grind beans. **Hope its STRONG! – because I have to get up in three hours.**

Gathered up all tax docs for appt tomorrow.

Thursday, March 17

Good training by Mark Brown from Marin Co. FD

His point about **stress management** was spot on.

Read a good article on LinkedIn about ethical traits. I'll take a combo!

Went to tai chi. They moved the studio!

Friday, March 18

The Colusa Fire Academy finished up HMFRO/Decon tonight. All passed Decon. 4 need remediation for FRO. Good news.

Email from Chris Post.

I did not know he was the Butte IC. Nice that he was thinking of me. We need to do lunch.

Saw Andy Zuckerman today.

Will set up a Monday mtg with him to talk about Valley.

Glad I am taking this medicine to help me fall asleep.
My brain can shut up for a few hours.

Saturday, March 19

Schatze just gave me a dirty look. I think because I took my blanket away from her! Silly dog!

Nice day today.
Academy students are improving

Glad Gilbert showed up today so I could **express my concern** about the $ factor.

Just chilled in my recliner tonight in front of the fireplace, catching up on The Voice.

And I get to sleep in a bit tomorrow.

Sunday, March 20

Test day at Academy.
Most passed. Some have retakes.
They got rained on doing hose lays in morning.

The Academy was an ambitious undertaking. My Bold Move?

Took Vitamin D this morning. Felt better the rest of the day?

Is that why I have been dragging recently?

Reading FB posts by Karl Parker since the Valley Fire has been **soothing**. Hope to meet him someday to thank him.

Monday, March 21

Not sure where I will go after retirement, but somehow I want to help rebuild the south county.

I know the book is the first step. It will help the SLC FF's.

I had some ideas immediately after the fire, just not the strength to follow through.

Like – ask Coach Nancy Leiberman to do a Basketball Clinic in Middletown (for the girls)

Or how about Dean Jacobs to do a program at the elementary school? How would I get the school to agree?

What about a student leadership program?

Had my first HPC session today with Michelle (Hujiev) for an orientation session. It was far-reaching and challenging so – the journaling for vision (see above) came out of that discussion.

So, this is my "new" nightly routine.

How can I help South Lake County rebuild?

Develop the vision.

Gratitude.

Had my first HPC (High Performance Coaching session) today!

I can see this will be **a powerful tool to help me regain my greatness**. There will be lots of hard work to develop the habits, but oh so worth it.

I made it to the "office" today.

Stared at Section 2, about the MAYDAY.

Wrote it anyhow.

It had been a roadblock.

Discovered Dagoba dark chocolate bars at Hardester's.

Endorphin kick!

Learned a few tactful ways to say no. Thanks Michelle!

Tuesday, March 22

Asked for and received recommendations on public speaking'

[Roger Love. Brian Tracy. Les Brown. Tony Robbins. Time to Shine podcast]

Wednesday, March 23

Listened to lots of 9-1-1 calls for Valley Fire

My heroes.

The men and women at SHECC

Onslaught of stressful calls. For HOURS.

Stressed out evacuees mad as hell

People about to lose everything

Lost connections…

Heroes all…

- Chris Veilluex
- Shelly Putnam
- Ryan Isham
- Julie Bradley
- Will Shunk

I will nominate them for the Superior Accomplishment Award.

How do you broadcast evacuation info to such a wide, diverse population in that terrain? What education needs to occur?

How do you respond to that without being **hypervigilant**?

Gratitude.

To my ECC peeps!

For the guys at KC who helped Cheri Lynn get her groove.

For Renee, for figuring out a financial issue.

For Lauren, crunching numbers for my buy-out.

Diane cooked yummy salmon burgers.

And the dogs weren't horribly obnoxious.

My irises and vinca are blooming.

I confirmed the location of the "House that Love Built 2.0" on Cobb. Hope to meet Karl Parker soon.

Thursday, March 24

Thought of another book/more books to write today

"Living the Stressed Out Life"

"Dancing with the Devil of FF PTSD"

12 step AA-> 12 step self-help for FF PTSD

Challenge Dr. Amen to do SPECT study on FF PTSD

Something, anything to remove/reduce the stigma

Gratitude.

Spent some time outside validating data points.

Walked in the woods.

Had a great conversation with Bert.

Looking forward to brunch with Jr. on Saturday.

Read some scientific articles on fire behavior. Enlightening.

Finished coaching homework.

Difficult.

Made me think about who I want to be, how to be more present.

Coupled with Brendon's audio on the 7 parts of our lives, helps me to have a sense of direction.

I'm really getting excited about my presentation in April. Watched a couple of TED talks on stage fright. Funny!!

But I can so relate! Reminds me of Sparky's TED talk.

Lots of books on public speaking.

Friday, March 25

How to help recover in the post-Valley Fire era?

Youth leadership?

Today's high school seniors will long remember but I won't be able to reach them.

Middle school? Options there.

Just think of all the NY kids post 9/11 who have done amazing things.

They just need encouragement.

But wouldn't it be better to build a company that could employ people? Potential for growth? Build a better mousetrap?

Book printing.

I don't know.

Something to think about.

Gratitude.

Curt and I had a good talk over coffee today. Caught up on the family gossip.

Marianne moved in with Devin's family.

Tonight, after dinner, Amanda called and said Marianne was in the hospital, maybe a stroke?

Marianne helped the kids as they grew up. Devin and Art were best friends. Grateful that she was at Devin's house and they called 9-1-1 early.

Wrote another section of the book.

That felt good to get it done.

Karl Parker shared some amazing bird pictures on his FB page. Looks like there is some competition for his bird house!

Wildflowers are blooming everywhere!

Met Chris for lunch at Woody's. Of course, we solved all the

world's problems. He shared ... some problems. I am glad he feels he can confide in me.

Saw Steve Stangland today too. Short talk but good to see his smile!

Looking forward to our day trip to the coast Easter Sunday.

Monday, March 28

Too tired to brainstorm.

Great talk with Michelle today. Clarity was the topic.

My words: Energetic, Caring, Integrity.

Actions towards others: Compassion, Understanding, Patience.

Words of Success:

Tenacity. Open to criticism as Growth. Intelligence – smarter than the average bear.

Writing today went well, over 1000 words.

Now done with the first two hours!

Tuesday, March 29

Business stuff.

Scrolled through ZOOMLEGAL re: company.

Problem with using last name in DBA is association with cannabis, but I think LLC is probably the way to go. Need to check ARAG.

Thank God for Imitrex!

Nice chat today with Scott McLean and Daniel Berlant.

Watched Bill Lopez drop a tree today with Wally on the front loader, giving it a little push. Only 6 months since the fire, wood is already turning blue.

Thursday, March 31

Joe Fletcher came into the office to apologize for disappointing me. He knows I have a lot of faith in him. We discussed other actions he could have taken. Lessons learned. Rededication to study more, to be better. I still have a lot of faith in him.

Ryan Bennie told me the Napa Co. FD gear at Yountville was ready for pick up (for the Colusa academy).

Schatze is goofy! She just pushed Curt's CPAP off the bed.

Yesterday Parkes told me he wanted me at HQ, that I was the right person for the job. So I am all in for the Central Division.

Summary:

Being in therapy was helping. I felt like I was getting better (so did the Doc). The hills had turned green following the winter rains. The flowers, given ample sunshine due to the absence of brush, were putting on their best show in decades. I had a bounce to my step. I was thinking about the future.

The signs were still there, though. Part of me was in **denial**. I was never a whiskey **drinker** until this period of my life. My **insomnia** was chronic. If I didn't take something to help me fall asleep, I would be up until the wee hours of the morning, and then have to drag myself out of bed and into work.

If I didn't feel like engaging with therapy, I still had enough wit to deflect the conversation. As soon as I got back into my pickup following the session, I would crank up the stereo and rock out, **so I didn't have to think about what we just discussed**.

I was drifting into **a pattern of working constantly**, often six or seven days a week. Again, so I didn't have to think. I was "too busy" doing something else.

I was **not fully engaged with my recovery**, partly because of denial of my situation. At this point, I still had not been diagnosed with Post-Traumatic Stress, so I thought that I could stay at the surface level of my thoughts.

"The courage to change the things I could…" had not yet become absolutely necessary for survival.

QUARTER 2: APRIL - JUNE

Friday, April 1
APRIL FOOL'S DAY

Had lunch with Willie at The Spot. Saw Steve and Tresa Fistler there too. Then Willie and I talked about the fire a bit. Will meet him on the 11th to dissect it.

Showed up for class tonight wearing a Hawaiian shirt.
Got complimented on it.

Had a Subway sandwich before class. Ate with David Rank and Jon Deakins. Both good kids, excited about class. Using what they have learned back at the district already.

Sunday, April 3

Fell asleep last night so didn't journal.
Good to actually be TIRED enough to fall asleep.

Class went well today. Lots of improvement by students.

Earlier in the week had a discussion with someone at work. Side-wise compliment to me about being a chief, a real chief, not just wearing the badge.

Had a wonderful dinner tonight with Curt, Diane, and Mike to celebrate Mike's birthday at the new restaurant at the airport. Keyboardist in the background. Fun night!

Tuesday, April 5

Tomorrow Curt is finally having knee surgery. Glad to get it done finally.

Completed HPC homework on Clarity. Life is clearer now.

Found a person to do trust taxes. Lawyer said to wait on the estate tax.

Tai chi was good today.

Wednesday, April 6

Actually, the morning of the 7th.

Curt's surgery went well yesterday. Dr. Gansel was able to straighten his leg out all the way. The nursing staff at Kaiser is awesome, as always.

I started reading a Tom Clancy book...*Commander in Chief.*

Clancy died a few years ago. This is written by Mark Greaney. Still has the same "feel". Great story so far!

Read over nine chapters in one day.

One of the nurses recommended a local café on Piner Street for breakfast. My next stop!

Gratitude.

Something as basic as sleeping in my own bed tonight.

Piner's Café – as good as advertised. Lots of selections.

Crossed paths with Tim Thompson today at Kaiser (retired BC from Marin Co. FD). We talked about the Valley Fire – " hold your head high, Linda..."

Appt this morning with Dr. Kopp

Told her about anxiety attack when the time between our appointments was extended...

I didn't like to use the doctor as a crutch...Her comment about using Rx to moderate a health issue, doesn't make Rx a crutch.

Damn it, she is sharp!

The dogs were happy to see me.

Schatze sure is sharp, for a dog.

I was starting to slide into a pretty dark spot, and she came up to me, made me get out of my chair and go outside and play with her for a few minutes.

Lightened my mood for a bit.

Dr. Amen's brain survey. Brain Type 13.

Restless like a firefighter! Nailed it!

[Amen Clinics, brainhealthassessment.com/]

Advanced curriculum for ECC?

What don't they teach in basic ECC school that would have been beneficial during the Valley Fire?

Something like verbal judo?

Need to reach out to Chris Post – IC on the Butte and Darren Quigley – IC on the Boles Fire.

What commonalities?

What can we share before the next one?

Sunday, April 10

Curt is doing well on recovery.

He spent several hours in the recliner this evening.

Most everyone had a good training at Wilbur Springs today (Academy).

Giants took 3 out of 4 from the Dodgers!

I still remember how to start a fire engine!

And I am really tired.

Monday, April 11

Had a good coaching session with Michelle today about energy.

Came to realize that it is not only mental and physical, but also emotional energy.

Relationships do matter!

So, I need to initiate contact more often, like a couple of times per week.

Curt is starting to do better. He can get in/out of bed without using the strap on his foot.

Started Tai Cheng program this morning.

Foundation test was no joke.

Proved just how unstable my hip flexors are.

But I started and checked in with my accountability group and Sarah Wizner.

[Beachbody, Tai Cheng]

Now I am laying here in bed with my pooches. Schatze warmed up my side for me, although I do wish she wouldn't bring the wubble to bed with her! Crazy dog!

Tuesday, April 12

Coaching session HPC today with Michelle.

No! Wait, that was yesterday.

Silly! Tonight I did my homework.

3 areas of intention to improve my energy this week include walking 30+ minutes outside every day; drinking a healthy shake every day; and practice talking with more passion and gestures every day.

And then I listened to Brendon "Optimize your health" to better serve others.

I am grateful for the interview process today. We found a good mechanic who is looking for a means to serve others.

Tai Cheng is kicking my butt!

Really making me use those hip muscles on the right side. Ouch!

Jim Wright received the Medal of Valor today for his part in rescuing the Boggs crew. Still humble.

Did not journal last night due to hospital trip late night with Curt – post-op issues.

Thursday, April 14

Diane had the stairway redone. Bye-bye gold shag!

Curt is feeling MUCH better today.

I think I am sensing a pattern of negativity when I am tired. More emphasis on sleep.

I did put words on paper early this morning about the explosions in Cobb. Certainly not finished, but it was important for me to <u>start</u> it.

I completed Tai Cheng and then walked for twenty-five minutes. My gluteus maximus hurts! The plank!

Friday, April 15

Taxes are done. Thank you Joan Sturgis from the Green Family Trust.

Tai Cheng – week 1, Day 4 done, plus 35-minute walk including the courthouse hill! Legs really starting to feel alive again.

Enjoyed talking with Jeff Gilbert tonight. Strange dude at times but can't doubt his passion.

Saw a bald eagle by the library.

Saturday, April 16

The library event was focused on the **Oral History of the Valley Fire**. When I was practicing for it, I sounded like crap, unsure.

But once I got started it came easily. Of course, following John from Calliyomi Water District was a tough act to follow.

Elizabeth Larson's tale of her travels with Hector the Terrier was funny! I have two more potential interviews now.

[Lake County Peg TV. Know Lake County – Valley Fire Panel]

Had dinner afterwards with Linda J.

I told her I was retiring at the end of the year. Sounds like she will too now.

Changing of the guard.

That is not a bad thing.

And the margaritas were good too!

Got a text from Cheri Lynn about lunch time thanking me for all of the encouragement. I figured she must have passed her hose lay re-take, and she did!

Proud of her!

Monday, April 18

Visit the Dr. today (Kopp)

Discussed recognition or lack thereof. **Trying to not let bitterness in. Not my style.**

Seems like my leadership role is rolling into pulse check on the mental/PTS status of co-workers and friends.

Dr. recommended taking proactive stance at work for employee support **as we enter fire season. People may have increased anxiety**. Will call Davina to discuss.

Made significant progress on Powerpoint (ppt) for Thursday.

Listening to more music, rocking out to Sweet Child o' Mine :)

Happy groove this afternoon.

Had a good process going for work.

Had a good process going for exercise.

Now I just need to partner them up.

Common sense is not always common practice.

Tuesday, April 19

Curt got his stitches out today!

Another HPC session with Michelle. Trying to coordinate work with fitness goals for next two weeks.

Discussion on courage.

Exemplified on the Valley Fire.

Courage and Leadership go hand in hand.

Found pictures of early Valley Fire on Twitter!

Learned how to trim videos in Microsoft Picture!

Way easy!

Continued to download videos using ClipGrab.

Will have new neighbors at the corner.

The Landrums' bought the property and will build.

-

Wednesday, April 20

Got the PPT 95% done today for the WUI tomorrow.

Tougher than it sounded a few months ago.

Teeth cleaning this afternoon.

Glad they called with a reminder,

I would have totally missed it.

Had lunch and dinner at MDT today. Good grub. Good company.

Saturday, April 23

Happy Anniversary! #28

Spent a great day with Curtis.

We went to Fair Oaks to look at a recumbent bicycle he saw on-line.

He could spin the pedals only 2 plus weeks after surgery.

So he priced out the one he wants and will save up for it!

I weighed myself this morning.

First time in a few weeks.

Down an honest 4 pounds.

Itchy back – direct correlation to dairy/ice cream

That is an easy fix.

Jerry the cat lost a fight last week and has a very sore front leg. This morning I saw him come out of the pantry. He had spent the night there. So I fixed up his padded bed and put it in there for him. Poor guy.

I think he gets to go to the vet on Monday.

No double rainbow today, but that was after the Friday rehearsal anyhow.

Grandma Nerell got it right.

Our marriage has been blessed.

Sunday, April 24

Participated in the procession for LCSO Deputy Jake Steely.

He lost his life earlier in the week saving his son. The respect of the Lake Co. SO Brian Martin has for all public safety made this a proud day.

So many Law and Fire agencies participated it was amazing.

(I have pictures)

And the people lining the streets along the way, holding signs, waving flags.

Their kind words on FB.

Gratitude for a job well done.

RIP Jake.

It may seem strange to write this in a gratitude journal, but I **could sense the change in my brain as it felt like my anxiety was rising this morning. Knowing that, I was able to tamper it down somewhat so a little bit of progress.**

THE PROCESSION

The procession

The obsession

For a job well done

Leads to stress

Self-imposed

Puts us in places

We'd rather not be

Makes us dance

With demons and devils

Too small to see

But we must

The obsession

For a job

Well done

The procession

Monday, April 25

Totally different day

Driving through Pine Summit today. Purple bearded irises blooming.

Empty lot with meandering path.

Progress on Karl Parker's lot clearing.

Epiphany: memorial park.

Stopped by Ken Leuzinger's place.

Foundation is poured. Contractor pounding nails. Ken actually seems to be a bit happy! I am very happy for him!

Did some meditation

Good day.

Tuesday, April 26

Got to hang out with the emergency leaders of the county this morning at LCFCA mtg. Met new OES coordinator.

That was the highlight. Last night's earache returned in the afternoon.

El Gato was treated for abscess. Doing better already.

Cueto/Posey combo in the 8th. Got the strikeout.
Posey gunned down the stealer for a double play.
G-Men get the win 1-0.

Wednesday, April 27

Another good chat with Michelle about productivity.

Gaby made lunch for all of the "office professionals".
Very healthy and yummy.

Printed out the certificates for the academy.
It's been a good class.

Someone posted a video of a waterspout on Lake Berryessa this afternoon. Love seeing Mother Nature in action.

Annelise posted a time-lapse video of Mt. Shasta. Watching the rotation of the stars is breathtaking!

Thursday, April 28

Just got late word that four of my academy students will get job offers from the unit. As long as they pass, of course.

Went to Region to get some signatures from Shana. Apparently, the word is out that I plan on retiring in December. She was hoping to work longer with me.

Got positive feedback from not one, but two peers on my webinar last week :)

Saturday, April 30

Held up the standards of the department. Unfortunately had to let some good people go from the academy.

Attended Jake Steely's memorial today. Class act.

Dinner with the family at O'Meara's.

Dog curled up by my side.

Tomorrow, Graduation Day!

Monday, May 2

Nice luncheon at Station 26 for Lauren and Corey. Great discussion with Tony Martinez about the academy. And Dan Herndon I actually hope he gets a LT BC job.

Then off to the doc. Interesting discussion on key markers of success for potential firefighters, such as participation in team sports **(Note: an example of Deflect, deflect, deflect!!!!!!)**

Wednesday, May 4

Yes, I got up this morning and did the Tai Cheng L-5

Had a shake. Off to work

HPC today on Influence. Great session.

Different perspective on what it is.

Really feel like I am building momentum in *life*.

May the Fourth be with you!

LOL.

Friday, May 6

Really…it is early May 7.

Happy Birthday Dad.

Been missing you for forty years.

Blessed to have had you in my life for fourteen.

Vehicle accident at work involving one of the fuel-crews.

Very grateful that it was only damage.

No injuries.

I get to sleep in on Saturday!

And write the rest of the day!

Saturday, May 7

Got to kick back this morning. Enjoy coffee with Curt and Diane.

Was able to watch clan war - live! [**I was denying it at the time**, but COC was serving me well as a **distraction**!] Interact with group. Anmol started to teach me Hindi.

Went to 'office'. Research mode today. Transcribed more radio/ phone recordings

Went for walk to Thai restaurant

Chased down by Andy from England. He was with Bert the day of the fire. I told him about the webinar. He will get my email from Bert. Andy said he had a couple of pictures of me in front of Station 60 that night.

Thursday, May 12

Lots of reflection this week.

Talking with Michelle helped me realize just how strong I have been these many years:

- The Rose
- The Rock
- The Duck

The Duck?

The oddball of the group. Unruffled, but paddling like hell.

Found a Tupac poem about **the rose growing out of a crack in the concrete.**

> Did you hear about the rose that grew
> from a crack in the concrete?
> Proving nature's law is wrong, it
> learned to walk without having feet.
> Funny it seems, but by keeping its dreams,
> it learned to breathe fresh air.
> Long live the rose that grew from concrete
> when no one else ever cared.

Saw Dr. Ko today. Thanked her for the referral to Dr. Kopp.

Robert Avsec from LinkedIn shared a couple of links on developing digital presence.

Leading a cyber team [COC] is tough. Somewhat pleased in the quiet vote of confidence from the clan on my leadership style.

They honor the old guard more than they value the victory.

The culture of the clan is set on loyalty.

Sunday, May 15

Spent time this weekend with Salina, Isaac, Niko and Kendra.

Chris, Rachel, Bret and Hailey, Chris Sr, Cathey and Mickie.

Good weekend.

This last week has given me reason to reflect on my health. God gave me a gift of physical ability. I have allowed that to waste away. I will reclaim it. It is a source of my power, my inner strength. I need it. I want it. I desire it. I will have it.

The 5th question:

Will this action help accelerate me towards my goals?

Tuesday, May 17

The bedroom closet project continues. Grateful for the **cheap-ass screws** available on the market now-a-days. Should be done tomorrow. Curt is working on it, slow but steady.

Yesterday, I followed through on a recommendation from Michelle, and bought the Franklin Covey planner.

Back to a planner that works!

Enjoyed listening to BB's discussion on influence. Will definitely have to repeat that.

Also got up early and went for a walk this morning to the lake. Beautiful sunrise! Great way to start the day.

Wednesday, May 18

Breakthrough with Tom today. During his performance report, he entrusted me with a critical area of concern. Jon Lovie identified me as a mentor in front of his comm ops this evening

Listened to BB on Intention.

I am full of possibilities.

Bring the Joy!

Saturday Night (the 21st)

Sometimes this journal is about gratitude.

Sometimes about pain.

Misery.

Getting stuck.

Where did that brick wall come from?

No joy at work.

No triumph.

So why am I hanging on?

Work is so fucked up right now.

Retire.

Is that quitting?

Or ending the pain?

I don't know.

What am I grateful for today?

Took a nap. Read part of a chapter in the Clancy book.

Did my homework, part of it.

Today should have been a writing day. **No energy.**

Chatted with Fred (Flores) last night. That was good. Too bad he is in SoCal this week. I could use a hug.

Curt's comments about the minion cookies.

Cut like a knife. But was it true?

My head hurts.

I am sad. Lonely.

Maybe just drive the work truck over to KC and leave the keys.

Fade away.

Man, I am in a funk right now.

Sad. Very sad.

I thought I was on a roll just a week ago.

Hate working for (the Deputy Chief).

I can't sit at HQ 40 hrs/wk.
 Can't do it.

Not my job.

No real gratitude for the past couple of days now.

None at all.

Monday, May 24 (really the 23rd)

What a difference a couple of days makes.

The Boggs crew really stepped into a mess Saturday night/Sunday.

Today was a good day.

Great visit with Michelle from HPC.

I could really feel the energy I had for the discussion.

Afterwards I did 1st workout of T-25, took pic and posted to the group.

Donna gave me shit because I forgot to tell her I had it.

But it's all good man.

Accountability partner!

[Beachbody, T-25 workout]

Then I had appointment with Dr. Kopp

Explained the Boggs scenario and underlying current of PTSD/demons

Told her I was off the Rx totally for sleep. Took a couple of early morning calls and went right back to sleep.

Added exercise and accountability partner.

She seemed pleased with the progress.

Tuesday, May 25

Day 2, T25, speed 1.0.

Definitively feeling it in my legs!

Tiffany cooked a delicious breakfast at work today.

Started to engage with Shana. She's not just a visitor anymore. She will not be wishy-washy and that is a good thing.

Overall – a good day.

Wednesday May 26

Start the day with gratitude.

T25 is done!

This will make me stronger!

Staff ride for Valley Fire.

Almost didn't go, but then my curiosity ruled the decision point.

Lots of good discussion. Now I know what happened.

I am at peace with it.

Talked with Bill at length about Sunday. Reassured him that he did all the right moves.

That silverback gorilla belongs to someone else.

Got home. Walked to lake with Diane.

Legs officially dead.

Should sleep well tonight.

Thursday, May 26

I dreamt of Mom last night.

She was younger, probably in her 70s.

Too bad Shorty woke me up.

I think she was about to tell me something.

Friday, May 27

Interesting day today. Signed the final paycheck for one of the Boggs firefighters. Lauren Silva's last day at work. Moving to Denver. I will miss her smiling presence in the office. But her new tattoo looks AMAZING in person and we are now friends on FB. Wish her the best! Her new home looks amazing!

T25 Leg Day: Adductor squats made my legs feel like rubber. I think by the third week I will start to "nail" some of the workouts.

I will keep pushing stronger until the beginning of vacation. So 27 more days.

[turn the page...to darkness]

The demons inside are hungry
Their incessant gnawing at your guts
Is more than enough to
Make you angry
It would be so easy to follow
Their instructions
To drink, take chances
Set up a scene
To blame others, but really
Listening to them only leads
To your destruction

Instead, my friends, here's what we do
Take counsel in a higher power
Allow Him to carry your load
If even only for a moment
Reach out to others, your friends
Your doctors
Just knowing that someone
Is trying to help
Trying to help YOU!
Is humbling

The journey is not easy
Anxiety and anger are
Constant companions

But just keep putting

Your next foot forward

Living in the past is

A falsehood

That the demons inside

Are feeding you

They want you there, locked

Away in your own fear

It takes courage to

Step forward, to ask for help

An unnatural act

For people of action

But you must step forward because

The demons inside are hungry

Written by Linda Green
5/27/16

Saturday, May 28

Is it okay to be grateful for anger?
The Dark Mood? I think so
Because when I go there, the
Words flow from my brain onto
Paper. Creation. Words have
Energy. **Even though the thoughts**
Can be dark, they also carry
Positive energy. Understanding.
Peace.

So it irritates me to be angry.

Even though in this case it's driven by a known issue.

But I am finding my voice by writing.

God. Take care of Matt Lee.

May his final journey be peaceful.

Wrap his family with your love.

Amen

Monday, Memorial Day

Matt Lee just died.

Not even retired 5 months.

How to be grateful for that?

Two weeks ago he was on a grand vacation in Mexico with Melissa and some retired buddies from the department.

Tuesday, May 31

Had plenty of quiet "me" time today.

To contemplate life, work, and the grand scheme of things.

Schatze can read me like a book.

Had a fro-yo with Curtis

My siblings gave me some space.

Ultimately though, I'm 2 bad days from retirement.

And yesterday was one of them.

Wednesday, June 1

Another hot day!

Got my T25 done early.

Went for a short walk. It was already 66 degrees at 6:30 this morning.

Reorganized back of truck.

MDT FF's helped put all the pieces back into the tool box.

Had lunch with Renee and Jr.

Good conversation!

Billy is on board with surge engine project.

Finished reading chapter on FEAR in *Motivation Manifesto*. [Burchard]

Talked with Michelle today about PERSUASION

Lots of anger last week.

Sadness this weekend.

Today is just flat.

Working on being strong.

Not being dragged into morass of gloom.

Matt's death is tragic

But I need to bring my positive energy to help lift up my brothers. Chris in particular.

Talking with Michelle, I felt PURPOSE!

That allowed me to speak with PASSION!

I must carry that forward.

Thursday, June 2

Day long staff meeting.

Felt like I started to drift a couple of times, but I caught myself and stayed focused.

Had a nice conversation with Richard Klasner. Told him transfer to Delta was approved.

Gaby brought me a bag of loquats!

Both dogs at my feet.

Missed my workout today.

Drank a good amount of water today.

Friday, June 3

Went to Joe Baldwin's graduation from POST. Drove over with Chris Sr. and Jim Wright. Had a good day!

Proud of Joe too.

Grateful for getting the opportunity just to spend some time with Chris and Jim. Both good guys.

Curtis bought me some lactose free ice cream.

It was HOT today, so that was a nice surprise.

Saturday, June 4

Curt and I went to Upper Lake to help the NSFPD Support Team cook breakfast for their fundraiser at Wild West Days.

Got to see some old friends like Scott and Wendy Drew, Sherri Fitch, Jay Beristianos and of course, the entire Crabtree clan and the Petz's.

Took a long nap with the pups.

Sunday, June 5

Found my outline for the book so I was **able to get back on track. Finally.**

Had dinner with Jamie and Lorraine at their place. The baked asparagus was yummy!

Took my measurements today.

Monday, June 6

What am I grateful for today?

I am very proud of Mike Crosby for delivering the *Fireman's Prayer* today at Matt Lee's funeral.

Glad to have a friend like Chris Vallerga Sr. to share a day like today with.

Good to see several of the old Delta gang.

The only one missing was Matt, but he was there in spirit so it's all good.

RIP Buddy.

May Melissa be blessed with an abundance of love.

Tuesday, June 7

Election Day. We have the freedom to cast our vote without being shot. How great is that?!

Mike actually paid us some money.

Electrician wired up the pool pump and kitchen light.

Got my T25 done.

HPC homework – DONE!

Had a moment of great clarity this morning about how to train my BC's.

Wednesday, June 8

Paul ran a really good Safety Committee meeting with Chief Jones in attendance.

Another awesome chat with HPC Michelle.

Purpose – what is my purpose statement?

I learned that when I am off my "feed" my mood can change to negative in a heartbeat.

Happy. Joy. Encouragement.

Take the next step.

The day you discover your why.

Thursday, June 9

Geoff tried to stump me first thing in the morning – I stuck to my guns on Title 14.

Really started the day right with T25 – LEG DAY!

Really glad Lauren's puppy will survive its owl attack.

Good discussion with Chris Glavich on the shop program. Turned into a chat on kids etc.

Lovely talk with Renee on my way home. She is such a hoot!

Beautiful sunset on the drive home.

Friday, June 10

Quantifying the Negative – interesting presentation on actually identifying the SAVE. Paradigm shift for the fire service. Hope it takes hold.

Enjoyed my conversation with Paul today. Glad he is giving such support to the Boggs guys.

Took a good look at the "well" at MDT station. Made out of pallets. Clever idea.

Started to work on my "Purpose" statement.

Vim & Vigor.

I like it!

Saturday, June 11

Here's to spontaneity.

Sis and I walked downtown to the Soap Shack.

Then we drove over to Ely Stage Stop for a Blues Benefit Concert for the Valley Fire.

Great music and food!

Monday, June 13

Couldn't find my medicine bag this morning. Finally found it tonight.

Good visit with therapist today.

Validated what I was thinking

(not sure they are supposed to do that).

Very nice lunch at Panera Bread with Curtis.

Curt did NOT drive off the road and crash.

Very grateful for both of us.

Got my T25 done and recognized I have been **slacking off on Friday's workouts.**

Tuesday, June 14

I woke up.

Shana asked how I was doing.

Bert re-assured me that he had been in constant contact with the Boggs guys letting them know it's okay to ask for help

The Willits guy sounded like he was talking to a rock star, and he felt blessed that I had agreed to talk with his group.

The HazMat certs showed up.

Wednesday, June 14

Long discussion with Shana
Nice to know someone cares.

Had lunch with Greg Bertelli today.
Always enjoyable.

Made great progress on HT inventory.

Enjoyable training tonight with the Northshore troops. They were engaged!

T25 Total Body Circuit done

Thursday, June 15

T25 lower body focus is DONE!

6 drafts later, I think the surge engine policy is done.
Beta test tomorrow.

Finished my purpose statement:

To be mindful
> To live vigorously
> To be joyful, loving
>> And compassionate

To actively lead and encourage others
> To mentor

So that others can know that
> Through hard work and
> Dedication

They can achieve things
To have a positive impact
On the world around them.

Ok, this is version 2
I'll keep working on it!

Compassionate or considerate?

To actively lead, mentor and encourage others

So that they can know that through their own hard work and dedication,

They can have a positive impact on the world around them.

Friday, June 17

I get to work with cool dudes like Gino DeGraffenreid and Cody Parks and Billy Bauman.

Attended the SLC VFF appreciation Dinner last night.

Won Clint Eastwood wall art in raffle + 2 bottles of wine as a parting gift.

Jim Comisky gave me a VALLEY FIRE Challenge Coin.

He started to cry, heart-deep appreciation.

To actively lead, mentor and encourage others.

The purpose of my life is…

To be mindful
    To live vigorously
To be joyful, loving
        And Compassionate

To actively lead, mentor
    And encourage others

So that they can know

that through their Own

Hard work and Dedication

They can have a positive impact on the world around them.

Sunday, Father's Day

Had a nice breakfast with the Crabtrees. Curt showed off his bacon jelly.

We got some of the scrap metal removed from the back yard and pool area.

Killed enough weeds to fill up both totes.

Headed over to Chris Sr's for a barbeque.

First time eating chukar. Very tasty!

Great company tonight.

Really enjoyed it.

Monday, June 20

Presence and Purpose. Today's lesson from BB

Grateful that I can write about stress without being unduly affected by it.

I'm not going to live there.

The purpose of my life continues to be refined.

The momentum for the book is growing.

Tuesday, June 21

My morning walk to the lake was very peaceful.

Tiffany cooked a tasty breaded chicken breast for lunch.

My follow through on an ePay issue unearthed a bigger issue. Hoping it leads to a better means of auditing the process.

Curtis cooked a healthy fish dinner.

Giants baseball = football score

Read more *Motivation Manifesto* – understanding our roles and responsibilities to be present and display personal power.

Warrior, lover, leader.

Thursday, June 23

(THE BEGINNING OF THE FINAL DESCENT INTO HELL)

Attended Critical Incident Stress training today.
[Cardinal. What is CISM?]

Afterwards, talked with Dana the clinician for another 2 hours

COMMENT: During this **meeting I kept flexing/tensing my shoulder muscles.** Then I would consciously relax them. The cycle repeated itself many times throughout the training. **I was certain**

the guys sitting behind me could see me *HULK UP* through my uniform shirt, which prompted me to approach Dana afterwards for a talk.

Cleaned office.

Stopped by Justin Galvan's soon-to-be new home., will be beautiful when it is done.

Got home. Turned off work phone.

(Start vacation.)

Saturday – Escape to Hat Creek

Finally made it here.

Hope to heal some.

Yes, I'm scared.

Stressed, as Dave would say.

Had a good laugh with Larry German

Former arch nemesis from Fresno.

Things to discuss with the doc on the 5th:

- **Paranoia...just a touch**
- **Got startled at work...**stuffing envelopes and someone walked by office door
- In-service training...discussion on **administrative betrayal**
- Dana Nussbaum discussion
- EMDR

Scared. Scarred. Is there a difference?

The closer we get to "fire season",

The more scared I get.

Uncomfortable driving along Highway 20.

Looking at mile after mile of

Brush skeletons, mixed in with tall grass

The red bud is turning.

Short conversation with Luke at Eric's retirement

"Well, yeah, I had a fire or two go bad…"

Bullshit! I call <u>bullshit</u> on that Luke!

I didn't feel comfortable there.

Left early. Claimed Hat Creek.

Lunch with Scott when I get back.

Maybe on a Friday. More casual.

I just want the pain to stop.

The anger to go away.

Almost didn't want to come here.

But then I thought of one of the things that was said at train-ing, referring to those things you "used to do".

I'm a fighter. It's what I do.

Just give me a stick.

(Thanks for the share Roger.)

I cleared my whiteboard

I am a person of integrity.

I am blessed to have learned my craft from dedicated people like those I am camping with this weekend.

Summary

If the signs were subtle the first quarter of the year, that changed this quarter. What happened? I wondered about it for months. Not until the fall of 2018 would I "connect the dots" and place it all on the topic of death and family.

- Jake Steely died saving his son.

- Matt Lee, part of my "work" family. Gone all too soon.

- The van accident fortunately, did not seriously injure or kill eight more members of the department. (But I was thinking it).

- Curtis fell asleep while driving. We both could have been killed.

- The "brush skeletons" along Highway 20 launched me into something much more than feeling "uncomfortable". It was a panic attack. And I felt oh so trapped.

- And the hills were no longer their vibrant spring green color.

The month of May could be considered the pivot point in my mental health. The negativity became more constant. New, subtle symptoms such as paranoia and a startle response made their presence known. The Incredible Hulk jumped on my back and started to crush me. At some point of time during the first half of June, I crossed that threshold and began feeling the full effects of Post-Traumatic Stress.

And I hadn't hit rock bottom yet.

QUARTER 3: JULY - SEPTEMBER

Monday, July 4

I have been remiss in journaling these last few days. Vacation does that to ya'.

But, about those fireworks last night.

The illegal ones.

Not all affected me.

That first batch was okay.

But the second one, from another location, deeper and slower rhythm.

Too much like Cobb.

Third set, same thing.

Literally, my brain started to hurt.

Tonight. Fireworks at the lake. Bad enough that the dogs were on spin cycle.

But the boomers made the house vibrate.

And my headache returned.

Make them fucking stop!!

That mortar round made me jump!

It's gonna' be a long night.

Actually feel a tad nauseous too, truth be told.

I see the doc in the morning.
Much to talk about.

Headache is in both temples.

Maybe we go camping next Fourth, and take the dogs with us.
Away from it all.. like Montana.

I wonder if Imitrex will help the headache!

Independence Day
I am grateful
That my ancestors made the journey
To this brave new world called
America
And that by their hard work
And determination
I am able to enjoy the freedom
That I have in my lifetime
To become the best person
That I am capable of being
In America
 God Bless the USA!

-
Tuesday, July 5
Saw the doc today.

Went prepared.

Frustrated by the setback.

Encouraged by her engagement and willingness to talk with Dana.

Had a good talk with Curtis about my situation.

COMMENT: Ah yes, the "situation". **Amazing to see how I avoided writing the things that hurt. I was diagnosed with PTSD this day.**

Swam with the dogs.

Decided to **quit ETOH** for 90 days.

[**ET**hyl alc**OH**ol, or ethanol, is the key ingredient in alcoholic drinks]

Re-engage with the real world tomorrow.

To Lead.

Wednesday, July 6

I exercised today.

Did T25 Cardio when I got home from work.

Enjoyed phone call with Mike Ming today. I am glad Warren is getting the help he needs. (in reference to absence from online schedule)

Thursday, July 7

Got a new Bluetooth stereo in my work truck today.

Now I just need to figure out how to work it!

Grateful for all police/LE.
Praying for all those affected by the sniper attack in Dallas

Grateful for trazadone.
Tonight I sleep.
Screw work.

Saturday, July 9

Very tasty breakfast.
Omelet with leftover stew.

Met with Tim Ward in SR.
Building my village.
Thanks for listening, brah!

Decided to not write today.
Just relaxed by the pool.

Went to gym:
2000m row: 12 minutes 15 seconds
Just missed breaking the 12-minute mark
Chest and biceps

Sunday, July 10

"Happiness is a warm puppy." Charles Schultz
[Schultz, 1962]

There is a spare blanket <u>not</u> owned by a dog.

I feel better after talking with Tim yesterday.

I wrote today.

Listened to Lady Bianca – jazz music.

Monday, July 11

Root canal – **the tooth was dying.** Git'er Done!
Also explains the headaches on Thursday/Friday.

Chiropractor – only a minor adjustment this time.

Mike came home today.

Outreach to other PTSD sites and sufferers.
I don't feel so alone now.

Tried to take a nap by the pool.
Shower dogs had other ideas!

Tuesday, July 12

The cops caught the armored car robbers.

Curt sent me a lovely animated gif of encouragement
My mouth is finally feeling better.

Only using half a pill tonight.

Thursday, July 14

Good energy at the staff mtg today.

Had lunch with Todd. He talked about France's firefighting system.
We set up a lunch mtg for Tuesday.

Finally connected with LIVE HPC group coaching – Psychology.
I was asked to speak and shared that Calm is Contagious
(Scratched out Courageous, which I had written first)

Talked about words of intention.
Joyful.

Confidence/Competence loop
vs
Merry-go-round of despair.
 Then Mark talked/closed with
"Be grateful for the challenges you face,
[embrace the suck – my words]
because then you have a greater appreciation
for where you are in life."

Thanks Mark (Bailey)

Great coaching session!

Friday, July 15

Had lunch with Boggs crew and got to talk with Doyle. Enjoyed that.

Lakeport Friday night concert at the park.

Saw Arch and Sue.

Great conversation about home remedy for stingray sting (add heat).

Saturday, July 16

Listened to AW's story (Note: at this point in time I have no idea who AW is)

Amazing. Moral of the story.

Family is what it is all about.

Read Dr. Amen's book

Change Your Brain, Change Your Life

I am learning about myself and ADD. Helps me to also understand those around me better.

[Amen, Change Your Brain]

Worked out this morning.

Healthy body. Healthy mind.

Sunday, July 17

Home for the day.

Swimming with the dogs

Mike cooked dinner.

Tender tri-tip and steamed corn.

Drive-in movies with Curt.

Finding Dory.

The BFG.

Bring the Joy (YouTube) video by Brendon Burchard.

Monday July 18

Jr. called. Met for morning coffee

Curt treated me to a Verizon trip

Got new phone with all the accessories

Swimming with the pups

I did NOT take a drink today.
That is a BIG one!!

Tuesday July 19

Enjoyed the day with Todd.

Got to see part of his division.

Discussed OIS. Work to be done.

Responded to Foothill Incident.

First real fire I have seen since 9/12/15 (Valley Fire).

Initially IC, then OPS.

I need to practice 4WD in that rig!

Kind of an all-around good day!

COMMENT: First and last fire since Valley. Last of my career. **The other unsaid thing at the time was just how uneasy I was while on scene. I was glad to be finally released from the fire.**

Wednesday, July 20

What am I grateful for?

Absolutely nothing.

Probably not an accurate statement, but two weeks of headaches has driven me here.

Thursday, July 21

Jimmie Robbins called me this morning.

Thanked me for assigning him to evacuate the Philips Ranch on the Foothill Fire.

Timing was perfect for that.

The fact that it was his grandma was an added bonus.

Of course, having retired Chief 800 Jim Robbins standing next to me at the time, saying "my mom is up there", just added to the moment.

Anyhow, totally made my day.

Thanks for that!

Saturday, July 23

Once I got to the "office" and started transcriptions, life was good.

McCabe heard me say "More spot fires than I can count…".

COMMENT: None of the official tapes of the radio traffic that day included this comment during my Size Up & Report on Conditions.

I was beginning to doubt that I had even said it.

Realized that my right side doesn't seem to hurt/ache/feel inflamed.

Maybe my liver is getting happy?

Also, headache seems to be dissipating. Sugar withdrawal?

Now to start cutting out the ice cream.

Twenty days sober? Or is it nineteen?
Last drink was on the 4th of July

Sunday, July 24

Family & Friends Day.
Breakfast with Crabtrees.

Star Trek movie with Curtis (birthday boy), Mike, and Diane.
Also, saw Jamie and Lorraine in the lobby afterwards!

Chillin' by the pool after swimming.

Reading my book.

Snuggling with Schatze.

Thanks Dr. Amen for writing your book about the brain in layman's terms.

USMC Lunker. Brave YouTube on your path to PTSD & EMDR

Monday/Tuesday, July 25/26

Birthday brats' turned into the Bathroom Blaaaach!

Food poisoning? Stomach virus?

End result the same.

Monday – no solid food at all.

Tuesday – some soup, a banana, oatmeal, cereal.

Maybe 1000 calories.

Oh, and two Gatorades over two days and a lot of ibuprofen on Tuesday for the pain.

Here's to a good Wednesday.

Wednesday, July 27

Still pretty weak, but then I estimate I lost 8 lbs.

Yes, that is right. 8 lbs.

Lots of rehydration!

Too fatigued to even go for a dip in the pool at 105*F

Thankful for a feeling a bit better.

For having a nurturing sister and brother.

For my dogs.

For the 911 Help Site.

Not much else.

Thursday, 1:00 am

Thoughts are racing. Temples are screwing in tighter.

Angry at myself, when Upton left, senior staff quit functioning. I didn't have the strength to call BS and remind everyone we had a unit to run.

Angry that I hate going to the office and dealing with the Bobbsey Twins, or being ignored by them unless they need something.

Angry at how inconsequential my job has become. Seems more like the accountability police.

Angry still, I guess, at the denial of ICA $ for Valley Support.

Angrier still that I was basically kicked off the fire.

Angry that the unit leadership has not requested even once that I attend a public function related to the Valley Fire.

Angry, just angry.

Angry that he continued to buy drinks for someone who so desperately needed help.

Angry that this episode will fuck up two people I helped develop,

Not including some FF's who worked really hard to make it.

Yeah, I have a vested interest. Much more vested than dipshit.

Understanding, perhaps, of *why* Scooter was involved in CISM.

Angry that sobriety has brought clarity.

Angry that sobriety has also brought more vibrant and worrisome dreams.

Call them nightmares if you must.

Angry that two people believe I will benefit from EMDR and WCPR.

Angry with myself…Why? Because I dared to be great?

Okay, **two pages of venting before running out of steam…,**

only half of which I really have direct control over

Angry that I know there are things I need to do, my responsibility, but I ignore them with the blink of an eye.

That loss of control.

Because none of it seems to matter.

Why do I try, when it seems like I am only going to be undermined?

Or is that an ANT talking?

Thanks Dr. Amen! I think

But, you do matter.

If you're not sure what your role in the unit is, it's time to ask for direction.

From Shana.

July 5 is Day 1. 22 days sober.

Thursday, July 28

That almost seemed "normal". To just sit in Shana's office and just shoot the breeze about growing up, and both of us going "around" Mom. Lol!

Even got a somewhat complimentary email from Parkes today on a staffing issue.

HPC Group coaching call. Good lesson on strategy for book.

Bumpy start today.
But overall, pretty good!

Friday, July 29

Back to back fires – 20 plus engines
Just a bit of chaos.
ECC did awesome!

On my way home, had a fun talk with Gary Uboldi and Kyle Steis.

Shana texted – "Stop with the 'shit' magnetism!"
(Me, the duty chief)

Got to read more of *Change Your Brain, Change Your Life* .

I am drifting from my purpose.
Need to make a course correction.

First day since getting sick that I did not feel weak.

Todd responded to my earlier email.

Keeping him and Team 4 in my thoughts.

Unfortunate, private Dozer operator was killed on their fire.

(Note: the Sobranes Fire)

Sunday, July 31

After being challenged in group Thursday

"you're doing a disservice…"

Coach was right

I was listening to a podcast from The Sobriety Network (episode 31) on Saturday. And the speaker, Bryan Edmund, essentially made the same comment: "you're doing a disservice by not creating… what you're being asked by the universe to create…"

[The Sobriety Network, Episode 31, Minute 34:30 – 35:15]

You have the story in your head.

Someone needs to hear your voice.

It's a disservice to not share.

My weekend focused on strategy, which

has reignited my drive, and passion for this book.

I have a lot of work to do.

Get out of your rut, you're

Stuck in a different mode.

Stayed up too late last night.

Big lump of dog (Shorty) in the middle

of my space, so I curled up around him.

Maybe around 3:00 a.m. I dreamt I was being punched in the chest and I was falling. Well, I was. He was kicking in his sleep and pushed me off the edge.

Even though I was **punch-drunk tired** I still went for a swim.

My dreams are becoming more vivid.

Not in a good way.

Self-harm. Alcohol.

Angry outburst at work.

Make appt with EMDR tomorrow.

Monday, August 1

I was trying to update Lisa on estate bank account but **I couldn't find checkbook.** Curt helped me find it, **which helped to calm me down**.

Drove to MDT and met with Mike Wink. He's trying to work the system, in a good way. Always glad to see his smile!

Lots of focus during my strategy session today. Hammered out the next three months of reading, writing, studying, and researching issues that will help me to move forward with the book.

Challenged twice in three days on

"Inaction is a disservice"

By both the HPC coach, and The Sobriety Network podcast.

That certainly resonated with me.

No clarity. No progress.

I think I also want to read this new book I heard about today...
The Miracle Hour.

Called the Healdsburg doctor to set up EMDR.
Still waiting to hear back from her.

See Dr. Kopp tomorrow, for which I am glad.

I got to have coffee with Tim,

and I get to sleep tonight.

-

Tuesday/Wednesday, August 2 & 3

Dealing with the Cold Fire

Doctor visit went good. **Discussed my alcoholism**. Dry since the 5th of July. Expanding my support group including Tim and Mike. Met up with Tim afterwards. He is still encouraging me to attend AA meeting. Finally searched for local information. Will call tomorrow.

Thursday will be day #8 as Duty Chief, thanks to the fire.

Remember the group call on Thursday at 5:00 p.m.

Thursday, August 4

Day 8 as Duty Chief.

I am tired.

Shana is worried about me.

Parkes can't shut down.

Yes. I am tired.

Warren has disappeared from the cyber-world of ISE. His profile is still there, but he doesn't exist otherwise. He is a proud man, and I am very worried about and for him.

Tonight's group coaching turned into a one on one session with Mark Bailey on persuasion and influence. I will need to listen to that recording again.

"Dude", lol.

Actually, I do like his challenging style.

Hope to meet him someday.

-

Friday August 5

Woke up early this morning, maybe 05:15?

Bad dream. I had gone to Warren's house to check up on him. He answered the door, but wouldn't let me in. Then he appeared behind the screen door with a gun and pointed it at me as I backed away. **All I wanted to do was say "I'm sorry."**

"Sorry I let you down, sorry I wasn't there to save you."

Just. Sorry.

How do I recover from that thought?

I took action.

Tracked down Ming and let him know that I was worried about Warren.

Mike called me about an hour later and said Warren was in a good spot.

He asked what prompted the concern.

I generalized the dream and just let him know that the dream was very negative.

Maybe triggered because yesterday I was looking through ISE and Warren only existed in the profile – nowhere else, like he dropped off the face of the earth.

Last time I checked it at least showed his sick leave for a month.

Mike let me know that Warren was getting the help he needed and that he would be in a much better place afterwards.

That made me feel better.

Then we talked for some time about dream symbology. I wanted to ask about my dream but didn't.

Why do guns keep showing up in my dreams?

Anyhow, I felt better after talking with Mike. I was able to take a nap.

Saturday, August 6

Started strong. Attended first ever AA meeting. It was a birthday meeting, so I have my first coin for 24 hours of sobriety. They all seemed like normal folks to me. They welcomed me and their words spoke to me.

Ran into Linda J. and Jim W. at the tacquirea in Middletown and had lunch with them. It was good seeing them both. Jim left for other business. I told Linda J. that I had quit drinking. She told me Pete was having some health challenges.

I helped Diane with her new computer getting it set up to print GIANTS TICKETS!

Earlier in day I sent Tim a picture of my AA coin, showing I had finally gone. Several hours later he replied, "Proud",

but since the meeting I had slowly gotten angry.

Found it hard during the meeting to say, "I am an alcoholic" and having said it, I got angry for having become what I abhorred about my Mom.

Started to argue with Tim about the anger, stupidly.

How many people has he helped over the years with their alcoholism?

I have a roof over my head.

I couldn't even remember all the words to the Lord's Prayer. **How far have I fallen away from God?**

Sunday, August 7

Had breakfast with the Crabtrees, including Trin.

Finally got to meet the twins!

Went for a swim this morning. Water was cool, but manageable.

Took a nap.

Decided to go to another AA mtg.

Different cast of characters but still very welcoming.

Texted with Tim.

The journey is one day at a time.

Advised to go as the stress builds.

Hungry. Angry. Lonely. Tired. [HALT]

One is okay.

Two, self-check.

Three or more, get your butt to a meeting.

Feeling better today.

Where does *anxiety attack* fit into that Rx? (HALT)

Monday, August 8

[The beginning of a *really bad* week!!!]

Went to Sacramento to PERS. Got a couple questions answered. Made my decision (to retire). Submitted the paperwork, even Curt signed.

As we were driving out of the parking structure, had an anxiety attack. Heart palpitations, muscle spasm, eventually tingling in my fingers, primarily left side. This was about 12:30 p.m.

The sun coming through the windshield felt good on my chest.

Relaxed the spasm.

Read a couple more chapters in the Big Book.

The chapter for agnostics presented the concepts of reason, faith, and worship, as the natural design of mankind.

It is in us. Accept it and let its power work for us, to give us the strength and the power to overcome our weaknesses.

All you have to do is ask for it.

[*Alcoholics Anonymous*, Chapter 4]

Resentment, fear, anger; but resentment is the prime motivator for negative actions.

Make peace with them, for they are sick too.

What a shift in perspective.

Tuesday, August 9

Woke up still feeling punk.

Finally called therapist to discuss the situation.

Stayed home from work at her recommendation.

Took a nap.

Lunch by the lake with Curtis.

Tai Chi

Had a hard time meditating.

Finally focused on

Faith-Love-Healing mantra.

Walked to truck.

Smoke column visible.

Drove home thinking of responding.

Started listening to HT and noticed stress symptoms returning.

Turned off radio. If they need me, they can call me.

Earthquake 5.0 at 7:55 p.m.

The dogs, Shorty in particular, were not amused.

Wednesday, August 10

Whole body/joints ached.

Glad I have chiropractor appt today.

Lots of tight muscles.

Cause of Valley Fire released.

Electrical work done by homeowner.

I thought I was good with it. Like, months ago.

Mother Nature was a bitch, etc.

Seems like it circled back to "Who should I be mad at?"

Shoulder muscles were tensing up while I was texting with Tim.

[ABC 7 News. CAL FIRE]

3 positives from today

• Researched Lulu – self publishing.

• American swimmers kicked ass at Rio.

• Tim told me about a new Zombie movie with William Shatner – *Range 15*, a Kickstarter project with US vets

Thursday, August 11

Went to therapy.

A long session.

Friday, August 12

Went to work. I think, thought? The doc was right.

I could do one day.

Hmmmm, maybe not.

I called Scott late morning, looking for perspective from a friend.

Told him about the PTSD, drinking, and having panic attacks.

To do all the things I needed to do required a daily time commitment. At odds with a 2 ½ hour commute and the time expected to be at work. I don't trust my supervisor.

Choked up while talking with him.

He has my back, I am certain.

Tried calling Ming. Went to voicemail.

Couldn't remember if he was starting vacation this week.

After a late lunch, Parkes came in my office with my timesheet. I forgot to burn a day of sick leave.

He sat down and asked, "What's up?"

So, **as a person of integrity I told him about the PTSD, that it was messing with my head and I'm having headaches.**

He heard from someone that saw my Facebook post on retirement

"Take care of yourself."

"Why don't you take a month off? But that would burn your leave credits."

"Why don't you just retire?

You're not happy here."

No shit Sherlock!

With you as my boss

And did I mention the PTS fucking with my brain?

Fuck you!

You insensitive pig!

"Go home", he says.
So I did. **Sick to my stomach.**
Stopped in Middletown to get a soda
out of the prevention building.
Glad no one was there.
Started driving up Highway 175. **Got past the splintered post,**
What a metaphor for the whole fucking situation!

Mike Ming called. I pulled over so we could talk.
WCPR – we need to talk.
He gave me Nick's number.
Peer counselor and intake guy.
We talked more.
Told him I had talked already with Scott and Parkes,
and if I weren't in uniform and driving the department rig
right then I would already be in a bar.

We talked some more, and I felt better after talking with him.

When I got home, I called Nick.
We talked,
and I felt better.

So, I didn't have that drink.
I did go out with Curt to the concert in the park with the Decades band and had an awesome time,

in spite of the poor excuse for nachos from Taco Bell.

Very bumpy day. I don't know if this is the last day I will ever wear my uniform again,

and that makes me sad.

Not how I wanted to go out.

I suffered a brain injury,

caused by psychological stressors.

It will take hard work to heal, but I am determined to do so.

So that others can know that through their own hard work and determination, they too can have a positive lasting impact on the world around them.

Live into your purpose, Linda.

Live into your purpose.

Live. Into. Your. Purpose.

Sunday, August 14

Liability.

So my career has boiled down to

I have become a liability.

My more reasonable side can understand the rationale.

My behavior has tailed off.

Can't tell if it's the alcohol or the PTSD, or a horrible combination of the two.

You don't want to be here.
Why don't you just retire?

You're a liability.
Thirty-two years, spread out over thirty-seven fire seasons.

And I'm a liability.

Tell that to Lower Lake.

I feel like a caged rat with the fire in Lower Lake.
I also feel forgotten.
My folks have checked in with routine things.
I don't know my work status.

You're a liability.
I don't think so, not on the fireground.
I may be worthless at the office, but not on the fireground.

I am not a liability.
I have thirty-two years of operational experience.
I am an asset.

I don't want to be here.
If *here* means under the micro-management of one particular chief, that would be correct.

If *here* means working for the Unit Chief, Shana Jones, and being able to have lunch and just chat;

that's another thing.

If *here* means **working someplace with no moral support from upper management,**

That is correct.

If *here* means **working someplace**

that doesn't care about the PEOPLE,

the *most* valuable asset this department has;

then you're right.

I don't want to be there.

I don't want to be someplace

where I am told to "'Just retire".

That came across as

"Get the fuck out of here".

That is how I received the message.

Wednesday, August 17

After a cooling off period, I talked with Donna & Fish.

Even Bro played devil's advocate.

Spent an hour last night texting with Davina.

Talked with Scott and Shana this morning.

They both started off by apologizing for that chief.

I told Shana that the fact that two chiefs, within five minutes, both felt it necessary to *apologize* for him, was an indicator that something was very wrong.

Sorry, but I was pretty worked up and almost started drinking again that day.

The fact that I was in the department truck and uniform prevented it, at least until I got home.

Thank God Mike Ming called me while I was still in Cobb.

and gave me Nick's number.

They both talked me down.

Doctor appt on Tuesday started with a bang.

Asked the doc upfront if I was fit for duty.

Yes, for firefighting.

Bigger issue is administrative betrayal.

I'm not on the far extreme of PTSD.

Discussed triggers.

I identified dipshit as a trigger.

I nut up every time I'm around him.

Control? May be the issue.

I don't worship him, kiss his ass, etc.

Now getting into the real work of counseling.

Family roots.

I don't think we have hit the mark yet.

Had lunch with Tim.

Good discussion. Funny at times.

My unofficial sponsor for now.

Went to a couple of meetings earlier this week.

12^3 on Monday and Cotton Ball on Tuesday.

They will become part of my regular agenda.

Finally, though, this morning, after talking with both Scott and Shana,

the right thing for me to do is to step away.

Burn sick leave and focus on healing myself.

It is the proper and best next step for me.

Thursday, August 18

Met with Shana for two hours.

She is very concerned about me.

Almost too much, but she cares and that is awesome. Part of my herd.

Todd called unexpectedly this evening and said he had been thinking of me since yesterday.

I told him what was going on.

He offered strong support and encouragement.

Part of my herd.

Called my five peeps to let them know I would be off for a while.

Closed some loops for them.

Secondary herd.

Mark Gradek sent me a text message, heard I was going to be off for a while, probably from Todd. Told him what was happening.

The book Davina recommended

The Rite of Return...

Great read. Has good info on how the brain functions and dysfunctions due to PTSD.

[Lansing, 2012]

Late last night I shared some meeting info (for 1st responders) with Matt Shobert [Butters the PTSD Dog on Facebook]. He saw the info when he woke up this morning.

Hope it helps him.

Need to clarify.

If I am off due to this injury, why do I need to request FMLA?

Friday, August 19

Diane bought baseball tickets months ago for the Giants vs Mets.

We went along with Doug and Linda.

Beautiful night at the park!

Giants won 8-1.

I think they are coming out of their funk.

Back in 1st place by a half game.

The Rite of Return is very informative. I need my herd.

There are things I can do to not **get stuck**.

EMDR can't come soon enough.

Tired of day-long headaches.

Swimming is rhythmic, which is good.

Had to take 100 mg Imitrex for *this* headache!

Late, late Friday night…

As the headaches abated and I started to doze off.

Seemed like a swarm of people were crowding in on me including a weird guy making faces. Did not recognize him.

Then later, the big fight with Scot back in 9th grade.

I was eating breakfast and he grabbed me from behind

I'm the shortest in the family, and I was surprised just how strong he was.

Saturday, August 20

Diane's birthday.

The return home did not happen today, but neither did the $125 Carole King play.

Had more fun visiting the deli by the beach.

Walking through the Japanese Tea garden.

Listening to the swing band and looking at the local artist's work.

The cannoli and cafe au lait in North Beach.

Spaghetti and meatballs at Emily's

All of this with Diane, Doug and Linda.

And a cup of chamomile tea.

Haven't actually done that before.

Anyhow, I am trying to stay in the land of the living.

Breakfast tomorrow in Sausalito and then home.

Go for a swim with the pups.

Here's to a peaceful night.

Oh, and we saw the new statue of Tony Bennett (just turned ninety)

We walked through the Grace Cathedral. Simply amazing!

Next time, I want to listen to the tour.

Sunday morning

Slept all night, until I heard the cat yowl, but I was able to doze off again.

Woke up from a dream. Person was waving a stick – a perfectly straight, square stick.

The more I thought about it, the more it reminded me of a dipstick, like at the stations.

The dip stick used to measure the fuel in the convaults at the stations. That's all I remember.

Another random thought this morning.

The days that I do sleep well, I have some _serious_ energy for the whole day.

Don't know what the combination is: better sleep, less negativity because I removed myself from work, or the body is healing from no alcohol. Hard to say.

I do know that reading _The Rite of Return_ has brought some clarity. Some.

Also, some action items.

Sunday evening, August 21

Had a late brunch in Sausalito. Opted for mahi mahi tacos and ginger beer.

Then we stopped at Wild Ass Coffee in SR then home. Good day.

Long weekend. High energy hanging out with a bunch of extroverts.

I learned from reading that PTSD manifests itself in two ways.
Anxiety/panic and anger.
I seem to lean heavily towards the anger model.

I am sorry I called Parkes "evil personified" when I was talking with Shana, but it seems he is **lightning rod** for now.

Chiropractor in the morning.

Then I need to figure out my *new* schedule.

To maximize my healing process.

Rest. Weights. Swimming. Tai chi. Meditation. Walking. AA. Therapy.

Time with my "herd".

I still regret how my last day in uniform went.

Because that led to Saturday, and the chief **saying he couldn't accept the liability of me responding to the Clayton Fire.**

Made me feel pretty fucking worthless.

Why did you wait until there was smoke in the air to make that determination?

Let it go. You're getting angry just thinking about it.

Monday, August 22

"It is a good day to live."

(*Helen @ 12^3 mtg. *not her real name, to protect her anonymity)

Being in solitude you can hear yourself think.

Being with others, you grow.

Moped around the house most of the day.

Emptied work truck.

Swam for twenty minutes

Had not attended a mtg. since Thursday.

I needed the meeting tonight.

Participated in reading.

Have I forgotten how to talk that much?

Brain is stuck in 2nd gear.

At least it seems like it.

Tuesday, August 23

Everyone, but me, had an early morning appointment.

So after I read some. And procrastinated on FB, I called an AA member.

It was good just to talk about stuff.

When I saw Helen tonight at AA, I told her that her comments from the night before, about **being in solitude**, had struck a chord. And inspired the phone call.

Twice today people talked about how they thought they didn't need the meetings. One person got weed whacky, another went gambling. Seriously. The meetings, the connections, mean something.

Attended Tai Chi today and paid Arch.

Also had a good talk with Mike, so protective of his kid sister. Love him!

Thursday, August 25

Counseling session. Curt attended too. Doctor signed me off work until October. Still have not heard from the other doctor. Apparently the message was garbled, so I left another.

We met with Tim at Lulu's. Had a good visit.

Went to the shop where he works at to drool over some pretty sharp cars. Tim gave us a tip on Costco in Rohnert Park. Only another five minutes. Not as crowded. And they have diesel for $2.36/gal.

Missed tai chi. Went for a swim.

Did part of the form in the pool.

Finished reading the *Big Book*. First pass through, now to start studying it. I think I will take Athena up on her offer to be my temporary sponsor.

The Giants beat the Dodgers.

Matt Moore lost his no-hit bid in the bottom of the 9th with 2 out. Bummer! But he pitched great.

Friday, August 26

Went to *Big Book* study group.

They finished up Chapter One. Bill's story - *spiritual foundation* is a key step to recovery.

Finished writing Superior Accomplishment nomination for ECC staff and submitted to Shana.

Yesterday Tim said to attend AA four times per week.

If I start going to that PTSD group in Fairfield on Tuesdays, I will need to change up.

I think I have determined that the power pole on 175, viewed going north, is a minor trigger/irritant.

Grateful that *today* I could write skillfully.

I took a nap today while at the "office".

Saturday morning, August 27, about 2:45 am
Woke up from a nightmare
Unidentifiable mass pushing at me, trying to crush me.
So, I guess the nightmares aren't done with me yet.

Sunday night, August 28
Had a slight headache when I went to bed about midnight.
Rapid escalation to a full-blown headache.
Took 100 mg Imitrex about 12:44 a.m.
Headache continued to intensify over the next hour.
Very restless.
If I thought it would have helped any, thought of pounding my head against/thru a wall.

Took another 100 mg Imitrex about 1:50 am

Rested in recliner until headache abated enough so I might be comfortable in bed. Maybe another hour or so.

Monday, August 29

Shana called to check up on me. Had a nice chat. Glad to know Mike Wilson is coming back to work this week.

Lunch with Linda J. always a good time. Even without margaritas!

12^3 meeting tonight. Read a story from the *Grapevine* about keeping the meetings as scheduled. Will start working with Athena as a temporary sponsor until someone comes along.

Got a call from Laura Capinis finally!

First appointment on the 14th.

Tuesday, August 30

Dr. appt today. **Update on headaches and nightmares.**

I don't know that I can work for dipshit again.

Possible solution offered.

Refereed mtg with agenda led by C1400.

One option would be allowance to work on a couple of special projects instead of resuming previous duties.

Tim wasn't available for coffee.

Dog nurse extraordinaire!

Contacted Todd, my brother from another mother.

Lunch on Friday at the Thai Bistro.

Tai Chi.

Really harvested some good chi today.

One of my better meditations.

AA mtg. Beginner group.

Getting to like this group.

Next week is my two-month BD.

Curt is losing sight in one eye.

The vision care place recommended surgery.

May need an extra mtg or two next week.

Don't forget to call Athena

And set up Friday afternoon get-together.

Wednesday, August 31

Went to Sac and had lunch with Dan "the Man" Cavazos at the Tank House on J Street.

Oh, so good!

It was good to just visit with my friend. I told him he was stuck with me forever! Stopped by Junior's on my way home. Got to see the munchkins!

Still want a drink. Will go to meeting tomorrow - noon.

Overall, not a bad day.

Thursday, September 1

Today's topic: Anger

My selection at today's AA mtg.

I seek understanding.

Nice meal at Bangers in Lucerne, then a drive around the lake.

Tai Chi – meditation was excellent!

Curt's meatloaf was very tasty. Rice quinoa & chia blend.

Talked with Athena tonight.

My soul has a hole in it, and it seems maybe AA can patch it up.

Saturday, September 3

Met with Athena today.

First step forward on the twelve steps.

Such a good and honest conversation.

Challenging sometimes but refreshing.

Spiritually confused.

Anger driven.

Broken physically (brain on PTSD)

Worried about work.

What is my purpose?

Do I accept a *Higher Power* in my life?

Not just intellectually, but deep down spiritually?

What was that quote in the *Big Book*? (p. 63)

"God. *I offer myself to thee* - to build with me and to do with me as thou wilt.

Relieve me of the bondage of *self*, that I may better do thy will.

Take away my difficulties, that *victory* over them may bear witness to those

I would help of *Thy Power, Thy Love,* and *Thy Way of Life.*

May I do *Thy will* always!"

[*italics* are mine]

I opted to sleep on it. Those thoughts.

I also focused on the HYPHEN:

(a) Powerless over alcohol (HYPHEN)

(b) Our lives had become unmanageable

Separate but equal.

<u>Sunday, September 4</u>

I attended the Sunday *newcomers* meeting. When I spoke, I mentioned that I had skipped over the founder's stories and read through Section 2. I would read a story and recognize part of me in it. Then I read the next story and find part of me in it. And the next, and the next.

The alcohol, and the PTSD, made me an alcoholic. Force multiplied.

I'm lying to myself even there. All those things I recognized about myself, were already in place, before the PTSD. That may have been the tipping point, but I was already a *moderate* drinker, and was on that slippery slope.

As far as Part B, **managing my life, I fucked that up already.**

Very few friends,

Outside interests/hobbies,

Spiritual life,

Marriage,

Finances.

Alcoholism was cunning in sobriety or, as the therapist said,

"It is an insidious disease."

What was really happening?

A couple of weeks ago, as I regained some clarity, my thought was **"What the hell just happened?"**

So, **how do I climb up out of this hole?**

Athena told me to start participating more. Help with coffee. Greet new people. Speak up in meetings. When an opportunity arises to take a secretary role, do so. Give rides.

Be of service. I can do that.

Athena also said to keep a notebook just for AA. Done.

While I was studying the *Big Book* last night, I really took notice of the course of my problems.

Self,

Resentment,

Fear.

That is still sinking in.

Resentment is anger, anger, and more anger.

Brought up because I finally said I was having *ANGER* issues at a meeting this week.

I was angry today, so I listened to Tim (HALT) and went to a meeting today.

Today's Daily Reflections - *the key word for me was* **Reconstruction,**

Like rebuilding a war-torn town **or** *picking up the pieces after the Valley Fire.*

"Yes, there is a long period of reconstruction ahead…"

[*Daily Reflections*, pg. 256]

And it dawned on me today that perhaps this is part of God's design. AA will help me reconstruct my life (my unmanageable life) AA will help reconstruct my brain (my PTSD brain)

By providing the social support structure that has been lacking for way too long.

When Curt almost died several years ago, I was afraid I would lose him forever. That blew a hole in my armor, and I have been vulnerable (fearful?) ever since.

Clarity is a great thing

Thank you, God for letting me have some of that again.

Tomorrow - two-month anniversary!

And so begins Step One:

"We admitted we were powerless over alcohol

(HYPHEN)

That our lives had become unmanageable."

Monday, September 5

At a meeting tonight, one lady discussed her new-found under-standing of *pause*. If you're unsure of a situation, **instead of just storming in** and taking action, just *pause*. Wait and see what hap-pens. Think about it. Someone will take action. Instead of being the one who *always* takes action, because *I'm* the only one who can do it. (as she said this, I thought of *The Indispensable Tiger* from Super-vision 2 training)

The key word I picked up on was *willingness*. This has to be a willing part. An actionable item. Let go and let God, as it were. Ask for help. Take that step back, and *pause*, to reflect.

The way I look at it, I got where I am today by *my* will. And al-though some things have turned out okay, others have not. And is *okay* good enough? Did I fall short somewhere because of my self-re-liance? Have I been lacking peace all of these years because of my *self*-ego?

Did I lack resiliency (post-Valley Fire) because I lacked God? I think so. Because they talk about a spiritual strength and focus as one of the keys to resiliency. So, lacking God, my spirit has been broken. I recognize that now. I can no longer deny that it was part of the equation.

[Note: I have changed my mind since then. LG 2019]

Another section talked about *willpower*. As in, willpower itself is not enough. I learned from Jade Teta that willpower is finite. It can be depleted by so many factors, such as fatigue, emotions, eating habits, stress, and illness. So willpower alone is not sufficient to stop drinking.

We need the support structure of AA. We need to follow the steps, and we need God (as we know Him) to be with us on this journey.

Sunday, September 11

15 years later…

Went to Middletown United Methodist Church today with Curtis and Michael. The topic was *remembrance,* but the bottom line was the *strength* of the community.

We then stopped by Twin Pine Casino. They were hosting an event.

Then on to Station 60 for a moment of silence.

Then a *Remembrance of Gratitude* by those there.

Nice touch.

Hope to get a copy of the recording.

Went swimming with the dogs.

<u>**Monday, September 12**</u>

A year ago, today.

Changed a lot of people's lives., *including* my own.

<u>A day that started as any other</u>

Like I tend to do, I showed up.

Got beat up. Bad.

Brain. Too much input?

Sensory overload?

The images of my burned brothers?

Fear. For me.

For my brothers.

And with the rising sun,

For so many others.

The Price?

A damaged career?

Retirement, with a load on my shoulders?

A hyped-up brain, that won't take *NO!* As an order?

PTS

Post-Traumatic Stress,

Not a disorder.

An injury, unseen

Hard to describe.

Similar, yet unique to its owner.

The *Symptoms*, you ask?
Where to begin?
Headaches always lurking
Around the corner,
The least of my worries

In no particular order,
The disorganized mind;
Anger, rage, hatred,
Frustration and failure.

"Stuck", frozen in time,
Sounds and smells,
Fireworks, and mortar rounds,
Illegal though they may be,
Take me back to hell.

"You should check on them…"
Like I'm an empath on demand?!
I did what I could
With what energy I had,
But who was checking on me?

Paranoia. Easy to startle.
But it started with insomnia.
Three hours slumber,

Five, if I was lucky,
Within weeks that drove me
To the doctor.

Lots of questions.
She's a sharp one,
But finally convinced her
I just needed sleep in a bottle
Of little white pills.

I failed to mention
The nightmares that had started.
Couldn't tell you about the early content,
Just woke up, drenched in sweat.

She failed to mention
That she was going to refer
Me to therapy
She's a sharp one
She knew I would say *no*.

And so the dreams stopped
As long as I was taking that pill,
But the morning lethargy
Carried its own price to be paid,
By tardiness and *don't give*
A shitness

But as I learn how to

Take care of myself, to heal,

I also learn how to help others

With my similar plight

Tomorrow is a new day,

And a new year

It can only get *BETTER!*

<u>Wednesday, September 14</u>

Met Laura today - my EMDR tour guide

**We talked about the Valley Fire, my role,
what I saw/felt.**

We talked about the *retirement* discussion with the chief.

She flat out told me that EMDR is not a therapy.

It is a treatment, period.

Pretty much guaranteed results within twelve weeks.

We start on September 30

Focus on *the* discussion.

Test run.

We will both know how I react after this.

Had lunch with Jon. Good talk.

Really enjoyed catching up.

Eventually made it home.

Needed a nap.

Laura did say I would be tired following the session.

Might be two hrs. Might be twelve.

So I might have Curt drive me those days.

Because, Boss, I'm just tired of this shit.

Saturday, September 17

Attended Unity Day. Learned a lot about the AA organization.

Encouraged to continue with service to the fellowship.

Meditated this morning and reflected on the leadership wisdom provided by John Maxwell.

Finished the day in gloomy mood.

Treatment with Laura will start with my last day at work.

Hope it includes the phone call.

The _liability_ comment has me in the dumps.

Despair.

Downer.

Withdrawing.

I think my friends don't get it.

Only Junior calls on a regular basis.

Depressed.

Hanging out with a bunch of drunks.

But cannot masquerade the pain

With booze or pills, even if they are Rx.

Go the gym Sunday

Call Athena.

Kill some weeds in the yard.

Just don't give up.

Not a chance!

That MF is not going to win!

Sometimes I feel like I'm done.

Why bother returning?

Meanwhile, the retirement paperwork has been rolling in.

Going to work seems rather pointless.

I haven't even worked on the book since before the Clayton fire.

Haven't been to the office.

They say it will get better.

WHEN?! TELL ME!

Spinning my wheels.

Tuesday, September 20

Rest overnight in San Luis Obispo. On our way to San Diego.

Debated on following through with this trip.

But, I've been stuck in a rut for several days.

The change in scenery will do me good.

Told the doctor yesterday that I was **depressed** on Sunday, and thought it was a spinoff from meeting with Laura on Friday to start the EMDR process.

She told me it was okay to have an off day, or a day off.

We talked about me being upset with my weight.

Eating too much, like it's out of control.

Commented that I'm still early in the recovery process.

Offered a thought on the 5:2 fasting program.

One of her co-workers has had some success with it.

Reading the book now.

Sounds simple enough, but then I recall Brendon recommending an occasional fast so there may be some validity to it.

Hope to sleep well tonight.

Got stuck last night on the computer until 3:00 a.m.

First time in weeks I have done that.

Need to mediate more. And pray.

I think this is going to be a good weekend.

Thursday, September 21

Day one of HPA (High Performance Academy). The VIP experience. Totally worth it! Finally met my coach, Michelle.

During lunch met Samantha "Sam" Horowitz, former Secret Service agent. Survived September 11 at 1 WTC, and PTSD.

Very encouraging.

Need to read her book.

1600 people. Rockin' it!

Friday - HPA Day Two

So much, so much!

Fish called tonight!

Great to hear his voice.

And his encouragement!

Where am I compared to the beginning of this journal?

[Note: I switched to a new journal book on August 20th... I called it the Dog Journal, because of how the cover was illustrated]

On August 20 I wrote

"...Trying to stay in the land of the living..."

Just went on disability.

Early in developing sponsor/sponsee relationship with Athena.

Saturday, September 24

Today's guest speaker at HPA was Robin Sharma, author of *The Monk Who Sold His Ferrari*.

Great talk about *leadership!*

Brendon's "Productivity" presentation was *so focused* on the steps, the thought process.

My big *WHY* has transformed over the last six months from one book to two, and then onto a Foundation - FF PTSD support/grants to help them get treatment.

That is a pretty big *WHY!!*

Laughed today. *Real laughter!*

No ibuprofen today. Honor the suck.

And it wasn't that bad today.

I'm getting more from this HPA.

Able to focus on the meat and potatoes of the information.

I feel like I'm learning.

Great meditation today.

The strength I gained by learning I could start to transition into a meditative state even while Brendon was still talking for a few minutes!

This has been a very positive week for me. I feel good about myself.

Wednesday, September 28

Grateful for some quiet time this afternoon

Started to piece together my post-HPA agenda
- Book list
- Sunday reflections

Tomorrow, Dr. Kopp

Discuss my belief about the death triggers.

Tuesday night's First Responder mtg in Fairfield was fruitful.

I think I will alternate weeks.

Glad I met Sam last weekend. Very glad.

Called George G to pep him up. Will have coffee with him next Tuesday.

I asked for his help with the retirement selection because truly my panic keeps rearing its ugly head whenever I look at it.

This is my time.

I got this.

Counseling and EMDR the next two days.

Here we go,

On the road again,

Up on the stage...

Thursday, September 29

Well, guess my theory was right. Even the doctor was shocked. Made _her_ think.

Upset that she is retiring mid-November

Sense of abandonment,
Not that I need a crutch or anything
(says the defiant teenager in me)
(Thanks Brendon for that imagery.)

No one from work has called me in about two weeks.
Even when I talked with Shana last week, I called her.
Talked with Bertelli tonight.
Seemed forced.
Or I'm just overthinking again.

Real sense of _Fuck the World_ right now.

Hope this EMDR shit helps.

Now I have to find a new therapist. I guess Dana if no one else, but that's a drive to Novato.

Got a pallet of pellets today and a black ink cartridge.
Small wins.
The Giants won
Mid-size win.

No Trazodone

Friday, September 30

Had my first EMDR session this morning.

Brought out the pain, the loss, the sadness,
The missing piece of the puzzle from that last week at work
It brought some closure
Peace
Fatigue

Just go with it
However it worked, it worked.

Enjoyed a very smooth cup of joe with Curtis at Flying Goat Coffee in Healdsburg afterwards.
Probably why I couldn't actually fall asleep this afternoon.

Was able to get some writing done, as an experiment.

Watched the Giants beat the Dodgers and keep pace with the Mets for a wildcard spot.

MadBum! Win #100!

I _feel_ better.

Can I get an _AMEN_ on a Friday?

Summary – 3ʳᵈ quarter 2016

The final descent into hell. Hitting rock bottom, at least close enough to rock bottom to hurt like hell!

The root of administrative betrayal exposed for what it is – shattered expectations.

And then the cavalry rode in from unexpected places.

The suggestion of the book *Rite of Return* was a game changer. The role that an impartial third party took in explaining a difficult concept such as PTS was tremendously helpful. The *ONE* suggestion I can remember off the top of my head was to build a tribe to support you…to support *ME*.

Since that book was written, the science has been pouring in on the *IMPORTANCE* of social support. Post-Traumatic Stress is not a journey to travel alone with. Yet, the very nature of it drives people, me included, to isolate and push people away.

My determination to "stay in the land of the living…" drove me into action. Get out of the house. Spend a weekend with family. Go see things. Take time off from work.

I quit drinking because my therapist pissed me off. Originally planned as just a ninety-day short-term action step, I decided to go to meetings because I had nothing better to do with my time. I wasn't at work. Friends had jobs, so I couldn't hang out with them.

A funny thing happened though. Well, not really funny in the grand scheme of things, but I learned a thing or two about myself

that I had not counted on. PTS had clouded my judgement, especially of how much I was drinking those last few months. For the first time ever, I suffered moderately severe withdrawal symptoms. Those headaches in July could be blamed, at least partially, on the alcohol.

However, I also learned that all of my behavior from earlier in the year had a name – Post-Traumatic Stress. That meant I wasn't going crazy. Now that the *enemy* was known, a counter-offensive could be launched.

QUARTER 4: OCTOBER - DECEMBER

Friday, October 7

I was having a good conversation with Curtis. Sean called. End of our conversation.

I finished packing etc. Still Curt talked with Sean. **I was fuming pretty good. Couldn't find my glasses. Really fucking pissed off by now. While in kitchen let loose with some colorful foul language.** Curt ended his call to help me look.

As he walked out to the Blue Dodge, I remembered leaving them there. I apologized for the language. **But did not mention my displeasure at being second fiddle** to his son, who calls sometimes twice a day.

Not very mature on my part.

Tuesday, October 11

"If a person has cancer, all are sorry for him…. Not so with the alcoholic…. There goes *annihilation* of all things worthwhile in life… warped lives of blameless children…" (*Big Book*, p.18)

As Dr. Kopp said, '**It is an insidious disease**."

Today's Inventory:

Good to be back at work.

Bad - the pickup at Boggs, next to the wooden box, PTSD trigger.

Good - worked through it. Went to HQ. Productive. Was able to have decent conversation with the chief. Not his fault about the pickup at Boggs. **None of them could or would know that would trigger me. Even I didn't know it would.**

Still have headache though...migraine. Time for an Imitrex.

Sunday, October 16

I have so many journals going, it's hard to keep track.

Sunday Reflection

Tomorrow starts my first full week of work. That will be weird. **Probably will be exhausting by the end of the week.**

Last week – The 5 Pillars:

Productivity - started filling in my planner. Helped to reduce stress by knowing what is coming up.

Physiology - one Tai Chi session. Had a physical. Encouraged to exercise every day.

Purpose - had lunch with Davina. Shared my vision post-retirement. Worked on the *Get Published* training.

Psychology - EMDR again. **That particular thought is stuck. Been having more headaches.**

People - Talked with Davina. Mike M. called. Received email from Tamara but still need to reply. Accepted service role with Lakeport Fellowship - literature.

Improve? - Make that call to Cindy at City Fitness. Touch the planner every day. Read every day. Drink more water.

For this week –

My Calendar:

Back to work on M, W, Th

Counseling on Monday, EMDR on Wednesday

Lunch with Kathleen

Need to book hotel for EA

Excited about?

Lunch with Kathleen.

Finding out how well my brain can function.

Send card to Pat Ward.

Pitfalls?

Back to the grind (trap word).

Getting up before 0600

Traps?

Write "Serenity" on whiteboard.

Surprise?

Send that card.

Buy two of *Rite of Return* and give to Shana and Parkes

Check on B.

Do something for?

Thank Wilson for the slot at WCPR in December.

Challenges?

Staying focused at work.

Take breaks, walk during lunch, and breath work.

Goals?

Verbalize "Integrity. Vigorous. Compassionate."

Energy?

Build energy by exercising 2x2, Tai Chi, meditation and prayer, walking, and water.

What stops us? - The unknown.

Let go of?

That anger from two months ago. It serves no purpose.
You are stronger now.

Motivation:

Health – Vigorous. Need to engage stronger here.

Mission – another PTSD suicide reported today. FF/BC :(

Love – We need a date night. Friday night movie?

Friends – Keep calling them. **Any potential candidates out there**?

Hobby – Tai Chi. Show up and practice twice per week.

Finances – **Blew that opportunity** to get account on autopay.

Try again. Explain your circumstances. Part of learning to ask for help.

Spirit – Nightly prayer.

Have been praying for Parkes. Keep it up.

Adventure – What are we doing for Thanksgiving? The coast? Christmas?

Quartzsite in January? How long? Tuscon?

Wednesday night/early Thursday morning, October 19 & 20

Had EMDR.

Hobergs - war zone.

Sugar Pine Pre-school.

The kids weren't there.

They were in danger!

So was I!

But I paused -

That tactical pause,

And grabbed the PA mike.

I took action.

Positive action.

Getting pulled away to the Valley 2 Fire did not matter.

There was no guarantee.

Regardless of which direction you turned

Or did not turn

That you might have saved that man on Humboldt.

NO guarantee.

You did the best you could.

Considering the overwhelming enormous

Amount of *inputs*

You got the people's attention.

Remember that guy on Summit

That came out on his porch?

When you chirped your air horn?

You made a difference for someone!

Be at peace with it.

Be at peace with it.

Be at peace with it.

Let it go.

Let it go.

Let it go.

Be at peace with it.

Go in peace.

Thursday, November 17

Reconnecting with my emotional self.

Learning to love again.

Came to understand the depth of my love for Pat and *why* **that hurt so much to see him the way he was.** [Result of EMDR yesterday.]

Released so much energy.

So much negative chi.

The whole week was full of anxiety and I couldn't figure out why.

Maybe because I saw Scott on Monday? First time I have spoken with him since my collapse, crash and burn.

I don't know.

Anywho - reorganized the house a bit. Got my writing corner set up in the blue room.

"We are all walking repositories of buried treasure. Life buries strange jewels deep within us all and stands back to see if we can find them. The real question is, do we have the courage to do the excavating?"

[Mackey, p. 93]

Sunday, November 27 (after Thanksgiving Day)

Maybe I should get back to journaling the end of the day.

Seems like things are popping up again.

Like the insomnia.
Intestinal distress.

Tonight - temporal headache pressure.

The muscle spasm in my back.

Heart feels weird.
What was the trigger?

Anxiety about the marketing plan for the book?

Just how am I going to fill my FB with content?

Have I started a list? NO!

So start one. RIGHT NOW!

Note to Readers: After several minutes of brainstorming, the following list was created. All of them are things I "learned" or "felt" up to that night as I traveled my path of recovery. LG

- Grounding techniques
- Why meditate?
- Importance of sleep
- Stick to your routine
- Schedule "solitude" time vs **social isolation**
- **Triggers**
- **Your reptile brain**
- Name that Lizard contest
- Book reports
- Who is your **lightning rod?** More importantly, why?
- **Substance abuse**
- **Suicidal thoughts**
- Family relations
- Who is in your tribe?
- How do you pay it forward?
- What are your creative outlets?
- Do you have a word or a phrase to let your family know you're having an off time?
- What podcast do you listen to? Why that one?
- How do you forgive?

- About exercise
- **Self-care/hygiene**
- Support at work
- **Headaches**
- Rhythmic exercise
- EMDR
- CBT
- **Weird dreams** vs **Nightmares**
- **Wake up/heart pounding**
- Trying to be **spontaneous**
- Walk with nature
- Swing band in San Francisco
- Art
- Cannoli in North Beach
- Trying to **stay in the land of the living**
- Grace Cathedral
- Labyrinth
- *The Rite of Return* - action items?
- Chiropractors / massage
- Recovery
- **Reading out loud**
- Spirituality
- Residential treatment for PTSD
- Return to work options
- When to tactically withdraw from work to allow healing
- A word (or two) for supervisors
- Day trips to visit friends
- **Anger** management

- Tactical pause
- What is your purpose?
- **Anniversary dates**
- Remembrance of Gratitude
- Strength
- A day that started as any other
- **Sensory overload**
- **Fear**
- **Symptoms in general**
- **Depression**
- Just don't **give up**
- **Spinning your wheels**
- Change in scenery
- It's okay to have an "off" day
- Practice Gratitude
- Who is your coach?
- Encouragement from afar
- Your *BIG WHY*
- Laughter
- Honor the struggle / embrace the suck
- Learning
- Quiet time
- Weekly reflection
- Coffee with a friend
- Shared experience / common bond
- Music
- **Overthinking**
- Real sense of *Fuck the World*

- Celebrate the small wins
- **The first EMDR treatment**
- Date night
- Asking for help
- Planning adventures
- Enough for now
- Have fun
- Face your fears
- Code word for family-awareness of bad days.

Monday, November 28

Saw both Dr. Ko and Dr. Kopp today

Rx from Dr. Ko: "Have fun."

Like, *school's out for summer* fun.

Kids screaming in the yard.

Fun, with a capital F.

What the fuck am I supposed to do about that?

From Dr. Kopp

Still have blockage (maybe) regarding the fatalities.

Recommend that I re-visit *ALL* the facts before going to WCPR next week. Read the fire report. Who were the five?

That is going to suck!

Her thoughts: Maybe I think I was able to save 19,000. Why not four or five more? **Why couldn't that be a perfect score?**

Another observation of hers: **A year ago when I told what happened, my thoughts were incomplete. Rapid fire, like the way things happened.**

Today my thoughts were more complete and informative.

She quit trying to track all the names - I know a lot of people.

She asked how many did I think were impacted by the burn injuries?

I knew six right off the top:

- Both FC
- One DC to be retired.
- Another needs to go to the retreat.
- One FF with angry outbursts.
- Pilot on leave of absence.
- FAE, long-time friend, not feeling good.
- Another FF reported by a friend as drinking an 18 pack every shift off.

Name that Lizard! George

Red card. Bad days.

Code word...from *Uptalk* Podcast.

(Conohan, 2016)

Death takes a holiday.

I wish.

See you on the 22nd!

Wednesday, November 30

Had coffee with Jr at Howling Dog.

Hailey has more testing coming up.

Had a good laugh or two.

The Dozer Operator Group (D.O.G.) meeting was going on at HQ.

Jeff Maddocks asked if the rumor was true.

I confirmed I was retiring at the end of December.

He sincerely replied that I would be missed.

Jeff Johnson bought me lunch. He knew I was off for a medical reason, so I filled him in on the PTSD in general terms.

Decided not to listen to any podcasts on the drive home.

I was thinking about something Dr. Kopp said about WCPR. Something like **"I won't be distracted by the drive to and from the appointment. I'll just be there"**.

Also, something said in Laura's office, when we were talking **about that undercurrent.**

So while driving I was thinking about the 19,000. Had I ever really taken credit for that? For them? Their evacuation?

Well, no. That's an abstract number.

Go to a structure fire at a house.

I can see the family of four outside, being consoled by neighbors.

I can *SEE* they are all safe.

I can't see 19,000 people.

Especially when they were absent from the fire area for so many days due to the evacuation. **By the time they let them back in, I couldn't face them.**

And the criticism on social media bit too.
About the lack of lead time for the evacuations.

So, I couldn't face the 19,000 even if I wanted to.
Hell, I could hardly face four hundred unit employees.

But, I helped Dale last night on FB. Fellow PTSD sufferer.
He had not heard of EMDR.
Or WCPR. I will keep in touch with him.
It *felt* good to do that.

I really haven't got shit done at work this week.
More pre-occupied with finding a new therapist that is culturally competent in the first responder world.

Plenty of children specialists, female Latina, even a transgender specialist. A few EMDR folks. One trauma specialist in Novato per the SCIF list of providers.

None of them were also listed on the EAP list of providers vetted by ESS as culturally competent.

That list does not include the doc in Novato.

Even the name I got from Dr. Kopp isn't.

And looking at her website, I think she is too New Age for me.

[ANT Alert! - save it for tomorrow]

Thursday, December 1

Had a bad dream last night.

While at WCPR, a female roommate came at me with a knife.

Situation was resolved without injury,

But a guy led me off to another room. I had to dissipate the negative energy and punched three holes in the wall.

In the middle of it, Schatze woke me up.

I petted her and drifted back into the dream.

Then she woke me back up again and sat there looking me in the eye.

I finally invited her up to the bed and stroked her side until we both settled down.

Then I drifted back to sleep.

This morning I recognized the basic layout of the room as being the captain's room at the Kelsey-Cobb station.

Also, today starts the last month of my career.

How's that for a sobering thought to start the day?

Sunday at WCPR, December 4

Slow start.

Why the Fuck am I here?

Peer to peer as an "icebreaker" _SUCKED_!

Seven peeps, different but similar.

Recognized one of the peers from the meeting in Fairfield I went to earlier this year.

In a room full of people, we _all_ feel isolated.

Four cops, two firefighters, one dispatcher.

Four female, three male.

All fucked up in our own way.

Gratitude/Lesson Learned

I walked in the door.

That took courage.

I can't be empathetic to others, if I have not (at one time or another in my life) been empathetic to my own self.

I'm not the only one with an **alcohol problem.**

In my (and our own) fucked up way/path anyhow, we have all earned the right to be here.

Not sure how I feel about *that* **one.**

An exclusive club of dubious distinction.

Sleep, perchance to dream.

Let us see how this *Emergen-Zzzz* plus a cup of Chamomile tea works.

Not so good.

Monday, December 5

Happy five-month birthday!

Highlight of the day.

Presentation on the symptoms of PTSD

Thanks for the fuckin' reminder.

Slithered off to bathroom to cry for a minute.

Personal Trauma Inventory & Questionnaire:

Survey says…

Suicidality is at 81%.

Prelim round in the rubber room.

The shit is getting real!!

Two videos:

Terry Bradshaw on depression, and

Motivational speaker Charley Plumb, POW vet Vietnam, said
"Prison think **will kill you."**

Both combined - *there is hope*

Combined with my observation of the peers

…they are not a glum lot.

TO DO:

• Update PERS to service retirement pending disability

• Hire a workers' compensation lawyer - PTS is a sticky wicket

Took a half pill of Trazadone. Hope it helps take the edge off
tonight.

Resource reminders (EMDR)

Safe place - *Citation* Beach in Oceanside, all that visual imagery.

Trait - my integrity, my rock.

Backup - Grandma Nerell's *faith*. The picture from her 100th birthday party.

Container - rusty shipping container.

Grounding – hear, see, and feel (tactile). Box breathing

Friday, December 9

Home from WCPR

What a ride!

Visited Tammy and Steve on my way home.

Took a nap.

Light dinner.

Updated 90-day plan to include reading list.

Took meds, including Trazadone. Early to bed tonight.

I have been blessed by the gift from Mike Wilson – the early date for WCPR.

I have been blessed with six new members of my *family*.

Matt, Chris, Shawna, Marq, Kasey, and Krystin.

And my new sponsor in life,

Big Red.

Duty. Honor. Courage.

I have been blessed to have married my soulmate Curtis.

I have been blessed by the loving guidance of Ellen and Nan.

By the compassion of Nick.

By the support of all the peers.

By the spiritual guidance of Sue.

I have been blessed with a *renewed hope for LIFE!*

Yes. I have been BLESSED!

Saturday, December 10

Mugged by the dogs! Still hyper from me being gone all week. Lots of messages from the Honey Badgers! They crack me up!

Got to nap most of the day.

Went to both of my normal AA meetings. A member read from *Emotional Sobriety* about suicide, and he was the speaker at another meeting later in the day. He spoke of his own intent. Told him afterwards that what he said today meant a lot to me.

Going to the beach tomorrow!

I have been blessed!

Sunday, December 11

Slept in until about 8:00 a.m. Had breakfast then we took off for Ft. Bragg.

We got a bit of Christmas shopping done.

Asked Curt to use his Amazon Prime to order the books I/we need for homework when we got home.

Had lunch at Django's in the harbor. NE clam chowder in a bread bowl.

Once we got home, Curt was fiddling with his phone for several minutes, and I asked him if he had upgraded his payment card on Amazon yet, and he said yes (I thought).

After moving laundry, I asked again and he said no. **(I'm frustrated)**

He set the account up, and then I was able to order the books for WCPR work.

The dogs, especially Schatze, were being overly feisty.

I snapped at her.

Mike went upstairs.

Hmmm. Guess the honeymoon is over.

Overall though, I have been feeling fairly relaxed since returning.

Watching Sunday Night Football, had an **icepick migraine** in left eye.

Have not had one of those for a while.

Texted back and forth with Honey Badgers.

Sounds like everyone enjoyed their weekends.

Eleven more working days until retirement.

I need to finish the policy project.

Make a bazillion phone calls.

Monday. Reality Day.

Monday, December 12

Those darn Honey Badgers! Really lightened my load going back to work today. _Damn chipmunks on steroids!!_ Wouldn't stop texting jokes! I will need to mute them tomorrow.

Matt shared a God-wink this morning.

Had to wait until after lunch but finally got to give Wilson a big hug for giving me the gift of WCPR.

My shoulder/trap muscles have been sore all day. Kind of like my temple muscles hurt after EMDR last week. No longer tight as a board. They hurt like a muscle recovering from a cramp.

Big Red called. Told him the weekend was good. I was starting to ease into discussions with Curtis. Books are ordered. His support is genuine.

There is _HOPE._

AA mtg tonight…Shared my experience at the retreat.

Also admitted to me, myself, and I (connecting the dots) that if treatment does not progress at all while drinking then, given our brain's nature to turn to the negative, having even one drink can begin the backslide of both PTSD and alcoholism.

Then drinking will kill me.

Therefore, I cannot drink. _Ever!_

I don't think the previous paragraph is fallacious reasoning. To Drink is to Die!

I love my Honey Badgers!

Tuesday, December 13

Early morning: woke up about 3 a.m.
Bad dream.
No idea about what.
Felt anxious.
Drifted off to sleep, more or less.
Woke up again.
And again.

Finally got up about 7:10 a.m. Got into office about 9:30 a.m. Actually, somewhat productive on the policy project.

Went to Tai Chi, at least tried to. Arch is on vacation until January.

Fish stew - yummy. Cooked by Curtis.

I was hoping to get books today.

Talked with Todd earlier in the day. Compared notes on WCPR. Will do lunch soon.

Called Kathleen after dinner. Discussed Tai Chi as a training option for her.

Nine more working days.

Grateful for my nice warm fire.

Good friends like Todd and Kathleen.

Got a Christmas card from Chris and Gaby! Great picture of the family!

And my Honey Badgers. I think they are starting to calm down.

Finally!!!

Friday, December 16

Today is a gift.

EMDR is at the point of fine-tuning issues.
Now that I have figured it out.

Hopefully, fireworks will be fun again.

Yesterday I felt I had that _edge_ back. It was just for a few minutes, but it was the first time I could recall feeling it since before the Valley Fire.

Gave my info to the lawyers' office. Need to call back on Monday to find out if they will work with me or not.

Curt and I started working on the *5 Love Languages*. Generated some discussion.

Found a picture in Diane's photo albums of me and Curt from when we took the four girls to Marine World. 1992?

Hired Aaron Jameson as my health coach.

Mind-body connection.

Keto diet? Never tried that before.

Sponsor was coming down with flu, so we didn't meet today.

Sunny, cold, and windy.

I think it's WINTER.

Summary – 4th Quarter 2016

If the 3rd Quarter of the year was *HELL WEEK*, then this quarter could be considered the beginning of *REDEMPTION*.

I started EMDR, which made an almost immediate impact on my stress levels.

I returned to work, although on light duty. It felt good to know that the day in August where everything became unglued, was not going to be my last day in uniform.

I only had one project to work on. *ONE*, and some days it felt

overwhelming. Other days, I felt like I was contributing something of value.

As the date for my visit to the retreat approached, my symptoms increased again. I can attribute that to the nerves I was feeling.

The end of December brought an end to my career in the fire service. Also, an end to working with Dr. Kopp.

Life was in limbo.

So was my PTS.

SECTION 4

CURIOSITY & COURAGE

2017

CURIOSITY

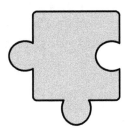

Post-traumatic stress injuries can happen to anyone. They can happen to firefighters, military veterans, abuse victims, and everyday people. These injuries can come from a single, sudden event or a lifetime of trauma. It affects rich people and poor; the young and the old; male and female. PTS does not discriminate. A fact that this middle-aged, college-educated, highly skilled, professional woman is all too aware of.

When I attended WCPR in 2016, one of the clinicians, Nan Herron, kept repeating this phrase, "Be curious." For the record, I absolutely hated that phrase. All I wanted that week was to be "fixed". Fortunately, that mantra <u>Be Curious</u> got stuck in my head like some songs do. Seriously, who can get the tune "Everything is AWESOME!" out of their head once that seed is planted?

Curiosity, though, is highly underrated by people suffering from post-traumatic stress injuries. The last thing we want to do is explore our own thoughts.

However, explore we must. The truth is, we have a bunch of <u>stinkin' thinkin'</u> to adjust. I'm not saying our thoughts are wrong. Some of them are highly accurate. Others though, need some fine-tuning. If you remember the days when televisions had rabbit ear antennae, depending on the time of day you had to move one of them a quarter inch one way or another to pick up the station clearly.

Our thoughts are similar. The trauma has skewed our way of thinking. Another way to look at it is the ol' brain needs a tune-up. Every now and then cars need to go to the shop for some maintenance. Cars are an investment, and to maximize their benefit, we need to take care of them. Our brains are no different.

Change the oil?	Drink more water.
Fuel up with premium gas?	Eat healthier.
Tune up the motor?	Be curious.

COURAGE

The "Lie" ability of Stigma

THE LIE

"Stigma" is thrown around with the understanding that it is bad, especially in the world of Post-Traumatic Stress. Stigma is a barrier to asking for help. Asking can be considered a sign of weakness, not only by the people that are around the person suffering, but also by the person themselves. Why is that, when asking for help is one of the hardest things to do?

I'm going to go out on a limb here and explain STIGMA in perhaps an unorthodox manner. I will share my own story here, because I think it will help to look at it in a fresh light.

When you have PTS, communication can be difficult. Your brain is on fire, especially early on, and triggers pop up constantly, sometimes in an area or situation where it makes no sense. Is it any wonder then that messages get jumbled?

When I first told my supervisor about my PTS, he was supportive at first but as the conversation continued, my anxiety was starting to spiral out of control. When he said something that triggered me, I was walking that thin line between massive anxiety and a full-blown panic attack. At that point I was done with the conversation and turned my back on him. I was in self-preservation mode, and that is all that mattered.

I only remember two comments he made after that point in time. The first one, offered up as he left my office, cut like a knife.

"Why don't you just retire?"

What?! And go hang out with all the dead people you just mentioned? Dude!

His next comment was more helpful though. "Why don't you go home?" Brilliant idea, I thought. Obviously, I wasn't going to get any more work done that day. Hanging out in the office felt oppressive.

After a cooling off period, a couple of phone calls with trusted advisers, and an outdoor concert with my husband, my head cleared up and I physically felt better. I slept well that night. The next day, Saturday, I spent some time reviewing some audio files from the Valley Fire. I had been encouraged by my therapist to do so, as a means towards filling in the gaps of knowledge I had about the day of the fire. Some people thought it was unhealthy to do so, but the more I understand the treatment modalities for resolving trauma, I now recognize it as a version of prolonged exposure therapy. Slow-acting though it may be, it was helpful, nonetheless.

That afternoon, the Clayton Fire near Lower Lake broke out. One of our newer battalion chiefs was on duty and had assumed command of the fire. I thought it would be good to respond so I could provide some mentorship on what had quickly turned into an extended attack fire.

My supervisor had other ideas though. Before I could even pull out of the driveway, he called me on my cellphone. "You can't respond", he explained, adding "I can't accept the liability..."

"I'm in a good space. I'm good," I responded, because I truly was.

My supervisor either didn't hear me or didn't believe me. He repeated his comment, "I can't accept the liability..."

Dumbfounded, I said good-bye on the phone, turned off my truck and went back inside, head hanging low. I think I told my family something like 'my career is over' and disappeared into my bedroom.

By the time I saw my therapist on Tuesday, I was a cesspool of negativity. The door had no sooner shut to her office when I demanded to know if I was fit for duty. She seemed surprised by my outburst and replied that I was. As she was an experienced police psychologist, I believed her assessment.

The damage had been done though. I had spent the weekend ruminating about my 30-year career wrapped up in a slimy ball of liability and worthlessness. I felt immense guilt and shame. Guilt for not responding to the fire. Shame for not living up to my own version of my best self. I didn't go back to work for six weeks.

You see, that is the LIE of stigma. First off, my supervisor, not understanding what Post-Traumatic Stress does to a person, passed judgment. Unfortunately, he did so when I was at a low point of energy. Telling me to retire was a direct frontal assault on my sense of SELF and I let it all sink in. Less than 24 hours later, he followed up with the liability comment. The virus of his comments burrowed in even deeper to my psyche quickly denying that I am worthy, and more than good enough.

The second part of the LIE is this. My defenses were weakened by the PTS. Like the hungry and foolish bass in the pond, I bit on the hook of his judgement, and found myself guilty of being a worthless piece of shit. With PTS, I believed him but without PTS, I knew better.

You see, there are two sides to stigma. The first rightfully belongs to the person passing judgement. The perception of the receiver is on the other side of that coin. In a healthier state of mind, like I'm in now, I can reject his judgement, because I know it to be false. Everyone has an opinion, but that doesn't make it right or accurate.

The problem with stigma, especially with PTS, is that the receiver of the judgment is most likely <u>not</u> in a good frame of mind. That judgement finds a place to land and stick. It has the opportunity to grow into the malignancy that it is, because people with PTS are too busy fighting the demons of their trauma. Until those demons are laid to rest, the energy does not exist to debate the question of worthiness.

Even as the healing process ramps up, the internal debate is running in the background, oftentimes unnoticed. The only reason I was able to see it in hindsight was because I was journaling. The negativity that flowed forth from my pen was powerful. Even as I sought to reject the notion that I was a liability, my inner critic kept puking up the nonsense that I was worthless. My mind was at battle with itself. Is it any wonder then, that when my therapist asked what outcome I was looking for in an EMDR session, I couldn't think of a damn thing? I wanted to believe that I was worthy. I just didn't know how to get there again. The suggestion that I was "more than good enough" was often met with a lukewarm "yeah, whatever…"

BE RESPONSIBLE

What to do about stigma, then? All things being equal, the person with PTS does not have to accept the judgement of another. The challenge with this assumption is that all things are equal, when in reality they are not. Someone with PTS is physically and emotionally exhausted until they learn how to live with it and their treatment plan has time to work. What that means is the burden to combat stigma is not, and cannot be, on the person injured by PTS.

That puts the responsibility right back squarely on the shoulders of the judgmental. The problem with that scenario is this. The people who need to be receptive to training on this topic are the least likely to change their minds. This is no different than all the people I crossed paths with over the span of my career that just didn't "get" the concept of non-discriminatory behavior. For all the EEO trainings, annual refreshers, and case studies presented over the decades, people still got "stuck on stupid" and crossed the line of acceptable behavior.

Fortunately, several organizations have stepped forward to provide education on First Responder mental health. Some organizations, such as the Firefighter Behavioral Health Association and Blue H.E.L.P., perform that oftentimes thankless task of tracking and confirming the completed suicides within the ranks. Without their efforts, the scope of the problem would not be known. National and international organizations have stepped up their efforts as well. [See Resources section]

BE AN AGENT OF CHANGE

It is good that all of this attention has been brought to light. What is bad is the molasses-slow pace that the information is getting out to the field. Post-Traumatic Stress Injuries are not recognized as a workplace injury in all 50 states. It takes something like the gruesome Pulse Nightclub shooting in Florida to effect change in worker's compensation laws. Unfortunately, the first responders that actually responded that night, are not themselves covered by the new Florida law. (Moore et al, 2019)

Another area that I see the opportunity to improve is within the policy and procedure arena. Most organizations have written procedures that identify how injured workers are treated. Has the administration considered how that policy works with a mental injury, especially given that the evidence is very specific on the role of social support in the recovery process? Does the administration have in place procedures for the activation of a CISD, no questions asked? In other words, has the department removed the administrative

barriers to seeking help?

Just as there are therapists who work with the military community, there needs to be a wider and deeper pool of therapists who are familiar and comfortable working with the First Responder community. Too many therapists don't even understand the concept of shift work, or that firefighters don't just fight fire. Having to spend four or five sessions training the therapist on what the job actually entails, before getting into the trauma work itself, is extremely frustrating.

Finally, worker compensation insurance companies can change their processes for handling mental injury claims. When the claim is initially denied, it sends the signal to the injured person that you think they are lying. If you don't understand the impact of that, re-read the section THE LIE. Also, ensure your pool of treatment providers understand the work culture of the community you provide coverage for. It saves time and money up front to provide that cultural training. Then you can trust your trained therapists to spend those initial sessions determining if the injury is work-related or not.

The stigma of post-traumatic stress runs far and deep. Changes can be affected at all levels of the treatment process. Regulatory policies can be modernized to reflect current knowledge. California law still refers to the DSM-III (1980), for example. Administrative procedures can be enacted to remove barriers to seeking help. More culturally competent therapists are needed. Worker compensation insurance companies can, at least on a provisional basis, approve claims up front, allowing therapists to do their job to determine causation.

Change is inevitable. The pace of that change can be influenced by people who care. My thanks to the researchers who are doing the work to provide objective measurements of psychological stress. The stigma surrounding Post-Traumatic Stress Injuries will continue to exist without those tools.

FIRST QUARTER: JANUARY - MARCH

Saturday, January 28

Have not journaled in weeks. Don't know why.

Depression seems to be getting worse.

Don't want to take sleeping Rx because it takes twelve fucking hours to clear out of my system.

Trying to live consistent but the combo is making it hard.

I'm "doing things" but not writing. Maybe the schedule next week will help.

Why do I doubt so much?

Part of me feels calmer but part does not.

Schatze intercedes. Demands to be petted as part of the nightly ritual, and then she is gone.

And what was up with the ice cream?

I've lost 7# since Christmas. Had a good walk today.

I don't know WTF is going on in my brain.

Too fucking long without a counselor.

Why am I bitter about this?

Sense of "oh, you've been to WCPR, now it's all good."

You're a POS. Bullshit! Bullshit!

Bullshit!

I gotta call someone Monday.

I can't wait another two weeks to check in on myself.

Definitively need a JFU meeting tomorrow.
I'm antsy!
A bit of distrust.
Like, WTH, even my journal is rambling.

I sat down to write gratitude.
I got flowers in my yard.
The birds are chirping.
The sun was out.
Walked to the bookstore.
And what do I buy?
"Failure is Not An Option"
Because people will <u>DIE</u> if you do.

Watching the *Last Ship* tonight with Mike.
Yeah it's <u>acting</u>, a TV show
But people are "dying"
And I can't handle that anymore
Writing this page I can feel the headache coming back.

Dear God! I need <u>you!</u>
Lift this burden from me, please!

Sunday, February 19

Journal, it has been too long.

Not sure <u>why</u> I quit writing.

It usually helps answer questions.

Like, <u>why</u> have I been in such a funk recently, and why for so long?

Lack of therapy, any type since January 3.

Had a head cold.

Off my feed, in a bad way.

Continued stress from SCIF.

Can't seem to get on track with PERS for my industrial disability or for Curt's switch to Medicare plan.

My content creation has fizzled. Or has it?

Oh, and the Maxwell house got flooded yesterday, and another week of rain on the way.

So why do I feel somewhat energized today?

Was it the "call to action" today to survey the damage?

Was it because "we" finally got the tractor moved out of the swamp?

The fact that Steve came over and patched our leaky chimney?

Robert Avsec invited me to write a guest blog (or more) and introduced me to another PTSD 1st Responder?

Or is it because, like I figured out tonight, **I want to shed this itchy snake skin of PTSD and be done with the negative side of it?**

Where were you during the Clayton Fire?
Trying to rebound from a 5-day long panic attack.
Told not to respond.

Am I out of my shell now?
Because Doyle reached out for help?
And just 2 nights ago Amy's dad passed away.
A maelstrom of events for their family :(

Why the headache tonight?

So much to ponder.

Monday, February 20

Coaching call today.
Really enjoyed today's call!
I mean it!

Started first draft of my blog for Robert Avsec.

Talking with Michelle. I recognized that having "purpose" drives me.

Instills me with energy.

So I need to read and speak out loud my purpose daily.

Also recognized the power of the nightly journal.

Sometimes just to vent.

Sometimes just for gratitude.

Sometimes I get stuck and writing helps solve the problem.

Maybe not right away.

Somewhat like 4th step.

Put it "on paper" helps to bring clarity.

Discussed the life coach thing today also.

Helped bring clarity to key parameters I want to look at as I narrow down my choices.

But I really need to have it narrowed down to 2-3 options by HPA.

(In case Brendon has some killer deal going :)

I also realized yesterday/today that the Maxwell flood situation has not "overwhelmed" me.

At least not yet.

The first bump in the road in over a year that hasn't done so.

Maybe because of its "exigent" circumstance?

A touch of the familiar?

No idea.

But I have a cat in my lap, so I think I am done for tonight.

Tuesday, February 21

Got most of the flood insurance stuff started. More calls tomorrow.

I missed Tai Chi today. And tonight's meeting.

I really need to tighten up my morning routine and pay more attention to my calendar.

Couldn't get online this morning on my computer, so made a mad dash to get online for EA zoom meeting using my cell phone.

1st time on the phone.

It was crazy but it worked.

Which was cool, because I was actually able to help explain how to network with other bloggers to Arvin. This guy is amazing!

And then, just a couple hours ago I was catching up on the Expert Blog Academy course, and then there was a blog that really helped to explain it.

Shared the link to the group.

"Contribution".

Go back to see Laura tomorrow.

Not sure what we will talk about.

Tuesday, March 7

My first PTSD blog was released today on LinkedIn.

Somehow, I thought I would be more enthused somehow.

Instead I feel blah, numb almost.

But then again, what the hell did I expect?

Another release of a painful past. I said I wanted to do this but now I'm **having second thoughts maybe**?

I don't think that's it.

Anticipatory dread maybe?
No.

Thought it would feel a bit sweeter maybe?
Get the boogie man off your back?
Getting closer!

Seeing it in words.
Black and white.
The Fact of the Matter.
Yes.

And now I will find out how it plays in Peoria.

So here is the self-doubt
The craziness begins again.

You know it is the right thing to do.
The next right step.

So you feel a bit vulnerable right now?

Closer.

Scared maybe?
Could be.

You're a fucking firefighter.
You're supposed to be scared.

I'm a fucking WARRIOR!
I shed off the turnouts and have stepped forward.
**Honed to do battle with the evil empire of
STIGMA.**

Ok, so that doesn't sound sexy.

Quiet leadership.
It's what I do.

**It's okay to say
I have PTSD.**

So say it.
Not in anger,
As a matter of FACT.
Not in spite,
As a matter of TRUTH.
Not in regret,
As a matter of LOVE.

For myself.

I'm one of the lucky ones.
I'm still standing.

And I should be okay with that.

Saturday March 18
    Home now [from HPA]
    Went to AA, then Fellowship meeting

    Then talked with a friend for a couple of hours.
    Yeah, she has PTSD, in treatment already, starting EMDR.
    A good reminder <u>WHY!</u>
    I share my story,
    That glimmer of hope.

    But hell, I'm still trying to figure out my own thing.

    Like why the anxiety attack at the San Diego airport?
    The noise? Maybe so.

    Earlier in the week **the siren from the fire engine going by for the 1000th time started to get irritating.**

    Fatigue was a factor, no doubt.
    Tail-end of a 10-day trip.
    Kind of a solo trip, at least to and from.

5 ½ days with Diane and/or HPA peeps.

Not as much ME time as I envisioned.

Good reading today at the meeting.

"I don't have time for this shit".

"This" meeting.

That's why you need to be there.

As Burchard said last weekend,

"Who have you been avoiding?"

"What issue?"

Who <u>needs</u> to hear from you?

Make that list tomorrow.

Sleep well tonight.

Peace.

Friday March 24

Goofy dog. Night time.

As always.

And….she's gone!

Whatever.

Just put pen to paper.

Ordered some books to read, as discussed during HPA, right?

Leaders are readers.

What I'm really tired of is the swing between anxiety and de-

pression. Anxiety at the airport. Depression at home. Heart trips out whenever it feels like it. Can't ever seem to ever quite get my shit together. The stability is gone. I can schedule all I want, but I can't seem to focus in on the day-to-day things. I suppose they will get better. Someday. Maybe.

My ability to self-discipline on multiple fronts is practically nil. Even a minor bump in the road like the broken (rat-chewed) water lines disrupted the entire week. Why is that? How is that inability to stick to a daily schedule going to play long-term?

If I'm accountable to someone else, I seem to stick to most of my appointments.

And why the hell can't I get untracked with exercise?
Hopefully going to Pilates on Monday will help with that.

Life is good.
Life is bad.
Grateful the headaches are gone (mostly).
Wishful [that] the brain function,
The executive decision-making was back up to par.

Part of me wants to throw in the towel, curl up, and isolate the crap from life.
Even though I know that would be extremely unhealthy.

I'm tired of dithering around, like I had no purpose.
So, clarify your purpose.
Do the blog exercises to focus in on that PTSD piece.

Study how others have done it.

Who would you interview?

What questions would you ask?

What will you say to Pat?

What's your plan?

Beyond hello?

Set up meeting in April,

Before you go back to WCPR as a peer.

Random Thoughts

The parakeet Posts on/about PTSD

Fall seven times, Get up Eight.

It's okay, you are still <u>getting</u> up,

Not <u>giving</u> up.

I think, in the long term, the home office will not work.

Too many distractions.

But I'm not ready yet, especially financially to get a place.

That suicide post really bugged me tonight.

A bit too graphic, too raw.

Because I stepped away in horror from Pat.

They don't teach you how to handle that.

Like, how the hell would you, anyhow?

Summary – 1ˢᵗ Quarter 2017

What a way to start a new year, and a new life.

I slept most of January, by design. It took about three weeks of allowing myself to sleep 8-10 hours each night to finally begin to feel rested. One advantage of not having to get up in the morning for work. The sleep was good. The lack of routine was not.

The lack of therapy was definitely a step backwards. It wasn't by choice though. My first therapist moved her practice out of the area. My new therapist had a health issue, and her own doctor was dragging his feet on releasing her back to work.

It also became clearer to me just how my brain was functioning. It wasn't. This began to consume me with concern because all that used to be second-nature was now a real challenge.

The flood in Maxwell was cathartic in a way. I had to get stuff done in a timely manner, due to the insurance process. It also opened the pathway to finally sell the house later in the year. A win-win situation, at least until tax time.

SECOND QUARTER: APRIL - JUNE

Saturday, April Fool's Day

Oh, Dan the Man

How I worry about you

You know that saying,

"You can lead a horse to water, but you can't make him drink?"

Don't be a horse's ass, my friend.

Make the call.

It's been nice having Melissa here.

Glad Devin came up to visit too

But I need my peace.

Nothing personal.

My PTSD has an ebb and flow to it.

I haven't recovered enough yet to be "up" all the time.

On Monday, I have HPC in the morning.

Joey's beta test Funk at 1:30?

Need to confirm.

Then Melissa to airport in SF.

I will have to go with Curt. That is a LONG drive for him, especially in the City.

I also need to call Pat by Tuesday. My word is my word.

The Honey Badgers will shred me if I don't

Hell, I will shred me if I don't.

The fear is gone.

Now you're just procrastinating.

The event is the anchor,
The King Pin

Symptom cluster.
Criteria.

No specific order.
Other than the event.

Sunday, April 9

Attended 1st Responder meeting tonight in SR.

Warren was there.

He shared a dream about him drinking.

I could only think about the nightmare I had last summer about me visiting him, and the gun he pointed at my chest.

I shared my concern about tomorrow's lunch, re-engaging with work.

Warren followed up with a very earnest discussion about his share at the unit safety meeting. Direct eye contact with me. I appreciated his share very much.

Another random thought…

I felt like I regressed a bit without therapy.

Now that I'm back into it, I *really* feel like I've regressed.

Or more like, I got the big rocks done with Kopp/Capinis

Now we are getting into the rest of that garbage.

Oh joy.

GRIEF

Homework?

What sort of fucked up assignment is this?

A ritual for grief? For bereavement? For my anger at God?

Or whoever fucked up the wiring job?

For the souls that died? The friends I've lost? How do you ritualize that?

For the winds that howled? The drought that persisted? For the gloves that didn't fit?

How do you ritualize all that to absolve the soul you weren't even sure existed?

Until you couldn't feel it anymore?

When the facts of the case made sense to the brain? But not the heart?

How do you forgive the life force of the universe for such rampant destruction?

Ah, but that was not the assignment today.

How do you grieve?

Pound nails? Pull weeds?

Light a candle? Plant a tree?

Why is the pre-school in the middle of this anyway?

No funerals to attend. No bodies to see. Just ghosts in the trees.

How do you grieve for them?

So you can be free of their apparitional grip from finger-less hands?

I need an answer god. Yes, you.

I accept the fate of my involvement in the whole scene. It was meant to be.

I've been reading Man's Search for Meaning.

As I read the death camp scenes, I read about me and my PTSD.

The difference that HOPE means.

That kept me alive, the belief it would get better.

Now I stand here, pencil to paper, asking for the how and the why. To grieve.

Show me the way Lord, show me the way. I'm lost at sea. I'm so lost.

How do I grieve?

Written on April 13, 2017

LG

Friday, April 21

Today's writing practice.

Just started reading Bones on paper or whatever that book title is. Writing takes practice and I have not been doing enough of it. I have found pen to paper is the way to go. It's more personal. The texture of pen to paper. The surface tension. The pen itself matters, I can tell. The fat grip is so much better. My hand is already getting tired with this pen! (LOL!! <u>Writing Down the Bones</u>, Goldberg, 1986)

Pente W?? Good for quick notes but not long-distance writing. Of course, speed writing takes more effort. I can slow down a bit. Contemplate a bit more. Let the soul speak. Of course, the book says a lot of junk will come out too, but keep the pen moving. Today's goal is 15 minutes. Probably still have 14:30 to go, ha!

People at the neighboring table talking about kids working. Playful banter really. Comparing notes on kids working for their parents. "You work your kids too hard" BS from others. But all the kids are now hard working, successful, respected in the neighborhood and community. Fun was built into the family. Camping trips and vacations. But taught them good work ethics. Proud parents.

"How do you get them to work like that?" from a neighboring contractor. "Well, sir, they either work or they don't eat, lol, until you're 18 and on your own these are the rules. I'm still responsible for you so don't argue with me. Just do what I need you to do and then we can go do something fun."

Looking for kids looking to be the best. Of course, that was their conversation, not my own thoughts, but that's life when you hang out at Howling Dog during a sunny lunch hour.

Note to self: sit someplace quiet when writing practice, Ha ha ha!!!

As if I really want to know what's in my head. I get enough of that BS in therapy. Or in AA talking at meetings, or with the Honey Badgers, or anyone else who gives half a damn.

But not from Parkes. He never cared. I don't care what Shana has to say on the matter. If he cares, then he can call me. But what does that mean about your thoughts about Pat? You called once. That is not enough to show you care. One card in 18 months does not show that you care. And that goes for a lot of your so-called friendships. Who is on your frequent caller list? There should be more. Texting doesn't count. <u>Call</u> someone. Just talk. That's how it starts.

Wow! Where did that come from?

Saturday, April 22

The irony of it is amusing. Striking me as particularly funny now that I think about the text message between Aaron and me this evening.

Yard work makes me feel better. Volunteering time at the retreat makes me feel better. The fact that I have been in pain because of the combination of these two elements is where the irony lies. I tripped and fell last Friday. Landed on my arm, then rolled onto my ribs. Thought I rolled through that okay. So well, in fact, I finally threw in the towel and went to see Dr. Erik to work out the kinks around the shoulder blade. Painful process, but totally worth it. However, now that <u>that</u> stupid spasm has abated along with the pain, the front side is killing me again. Under the breast. Four weeks for this to resolve? Great! I should beat MadBum back from the DL!

Sorry, MadBum, you are opening the season with a bunch of loses. Blame the front office but come back fresh mentally. The bats hopefully will wake up by then. Posey getting plunked the first inning of the first game. Fight through that. How much do you want it?

How would my retirement be different if I didn't have PTSD?

No way of knowing. No way of knowing how different my life will be in another six months.

Sobriety chips every month for the first year in AA. That's too fast for PTSD. I think you have to break it down in 4-6 months. So yeah, three months because that is how subtle the changes are. Very

subtle. **But even now, writing this, I can feel my heart start to trip a bit. So the question is why?**

The homework. You've been thinking about it all day. How about writing about it instead?

Hmmmm? as Kasey would say.

Why can't you look at your uniforms anymore? Why do you feel like you couldn't retire with dignity? Or is it dishonor? What about phone calls? Was talking to Scott about the fire, in particular Pat's injuries, <u>that</u> painful? Call a friend to say another friend was injured? No, something else.

The dignity/dishonor thing though. There might be some meat to that issue. "Why don't you just retire?" Wow. "I can't accept the liability." Wow, again.

We didn't resolve that. **That week in August, panic-stricken as it was, was about death. The messages stacked up. But I don't think we dealt with the dignity/dishonor/retire shit.** Higher priority than dealing with phone calls. **Dishonor.** That's the word. If nothing else, my writing practice will daylight some issues, good, bad, or indifferent. It is what it is. **I felt dishonored. And I'm furious about it.**

Sunday, April 23

What the hell is wrong with me anyways? We were having a good day. I checked Facebook. Saw Tom H's post. Pat Ward and Chris Stone got married today. I'm happy for them, truly. Tom's additional comment about being there with the "Boggs" family I think is what set me off. **I have no work family. I was dishonorably discharged. I know it's not true, but my brain is stuck on it. Fuck, I don't know.**

One minute I'm in a good mood. Then I started brooding

about it. Then I freaked out when Curt was speeding down the grade. Not like that's the first time that has happened. I was just speculating on that issue the other day. I thought I was past it. Well, apparently not. Add it to the list for the doctor. Is that connected with the drive down 175? Possibly. I don't know.

Was I lying to Dan when I said I never felt like a failure? Possibly. Probably. **I never wanted that to be my last command. No way now of getting back on my horse.** Riding off into the sunset, in a blaze of glory. No. Nope. Not happening. **Because I'm such a fuck up. The Facebook comments following the fire were scathing in their criticism of the evacuation. Coming from people I know, they cut particularly deep.**

What I don't understand is why the disengagement of me? Not allowed to stay on the fire. Even informally. Did I say something? No, I was too stunned, I think. I could make it to the debriefs. I could make it to the hospital. I helped Paul out with his dress uniform.

But **I have amnesia about so much more.** I drove around the mountain most days looking at the devastation. Absorbing it. Owning it. As the IC.

My responsibility. But was it?

What about the wind? God.

What about the drought, god?

What about the dead trees? god?!

Why?

I don't understand any of that.

The perfect storm on my watch?

Why me.

Why fuck with me?

Are you trying to drive me away?

Just when I finally figure out the soul connection?

I just don't understand that part of it. Does the Doc have it right? Do I need to stomp my feet and curse you out? Get it off my chest? <u>You</u> can handle it so how do I get satisfaction from that? How will that possibly make me feel better?

I don't see any purpose to it. Try to solve something by engaging in futile action. Like pissing in the wind. Or stopping that fire. Why did I keep going that night? What made me so special?

Pat was hurt. I kept going.

Had a **panic attack** at the pre-school. I kept going.

Couldn't connect with Bert? I kept going.

Plume dominated fire behavior? I kept going.

And going.

And going.

And going.

Until I couldn't go anymore.

When did that happen?

When did I **begin to shut down**?

When the **suicidal thoughts** first popped into my head?

When I **couldn't face the media**?

When I couldn't tell Shana about my PTSD?

No.

Way before that.

Before the brush skeletons.

Before Matt Lee.

When?

The Unit Safety Meeting?!

Parkes wanted a presentation on the Valley Fire.

I didn't have the balls to flat out tell him no. But I couldn't put

Bert through that. Or Todd. Or anyone else.

So I took one for the team.

I think that was it.

I had a hard time talking in front of everyone.

Crushing blow to my ego.

These are my peeps and I could hardly stand there.

False prophet.

I'd forgotten about that. That was in March.

Tuesday, April 25

Yesterday I did not write. Fatigue maybe. **Maybe just a rebound effect from being triggered on Sunday by seeing Pat's picture on Facebook**. Really, the first public picture of Pat since the fire. Maybe his way of reintroducing himself to the larger society? I have no idea. I will have to ask him. Someday.

But why did I not write yesterday? Daily practice is just that. No pretense, right? The process of getting the junk out of our brains so when it really matters, what we write makes some sense, or not. Hard to say. For instance, I can tell the difference in my hand grip when I'm pressing too hard, physically and mentally, as I write. As opposed to the more flowing script when I'm on a roll. The realization of this is bringing me faith that yes, I will be able to do this thing.

Today's discussion on EA Warriors about meaning and purpose and vision has been a constant theme the last few weeks. Which really highlights just how important is to have <u>clarity</u> on what we are doing each day.

So how does this writing practice help me convince people to ask for help? Because I can try different ideas here. No interruptions - hopefully. I will know as I write if what I am saying is true or not. If I can't convince myself, how can I convince others?

Words can be molded, changed, scratched out (well, not in prac-

tice mode), scrambled, rearranged, CRAFTED, to convey the right message. Writing for the sake of writing is just exercise. But writing with intent is another thing.

No scratching! Powerful things. Words are powerful.

They can make or break a communication. Used incorrectly, they can harm, cause damage, if not even kill someone or some cause. What if that cause was important for society as a whole? What if the cause I hurt was increased funding for the treatment and/or research in PTSI? What if the person my words hit wrong, kills himself? I have to ask these tough questions now, because the consequences - negative ones - can be so severe.

That's why I need the critical incident stress training. Above all else, cause no harm. Right? Unlike dipshit? I could write a whole course on just that piece right there. I could? No, I will. And it will be part - "get in your face" - don't do that to people! And part compassion, understanding, and patience.

Post-Traumatic Stress doesn't resolve itself overnight. So why be in a rush to brush off your employee who is suffering? Right? And how do you keep them engaged with work after the fact? Brush them off totally while they are undergoing treatment?

Case by case scentaio, really. The person may really need to disengage from work in order to heal. Yes, like you did.

Do you honestly think you would have done okay if you had continued working through September and October? Not a chance.

Hell, **my head was about to explode** by the retreat. Actually, surprised it didn't.

So, before you come out with your guns blazing, think this part through. What is your agenda? To help people? Or to fry all the supervisors out there for the sin of one bad apple chief officer?

But that's why you are going public, right? To stop that sort of thing? Yes. yes, it is.

My own **suicidal ideation was terrifying enough**. But I wasn't at the end of my proverbial rope either. Because I still had hope!

Thursday, April 27

I have been remiss in my writing practice the last couple of days. Watched the Giants beat LA last night. Morse hit a glorious home run to tie the score. His first at bat since his return to the team. Yeah boy! Christian Arroyo also hit his first home run, ever, in the big leagues. Welcome both of you! Glad to have you.

Last night I was thinking about writing after the game. Instead, I just thought. **Think. Think. Think**. I agreed to be interviewed for a department training video about PTSD for this year's Focus on Safety. [never happened] My story. How is that going to play in Pretoria? Right? The questions seem relatively benign on paper. Until you start thinking about the answers. I haven't even said some of that stuff outside of therapy. Now everyone will know. **Vulnerable**, most definitely.

Had an awesome talk with Joey in the afternoon to discuss his course that he was beta testing. He reminded me it was okay to be vulnerable. As I review, rehearse, say things out loud, that will help build my confidence and courage. There is power in telling your story. In sharing. And is this not also part of your purpose? To get people to ask for help, right?

Because <u>recovery</u> is worth the journey. Things do get better. But you can't travel that path alone. Share the load. Get a tour guide - skilled therapist - right?

Not a sign of weakness. You are already carrying a heavy load, alone, by yourself. How long do you want to carry that solo? Strong people don't want to share that load. I guess my question to those still working would be along the lines of:

"Hey, you are already carrying a heavy weight. Each critical call just keeps adding more to it. Just how strong are you? Unload some of that before you get the next heavy weight dumped on your shoulders. Do you carry the hose pack all the way to the end of a 15,000 foot hoselay? The entire pack? Plus all the contents of a brass bag?"

I know, dating myself here!

But really. You pull out a length somewhere along the way, lighten the load. How many bottles do you breathe down before you take a break and rehab?

Right?

You lighten the load on your body to help recover physically. **Why won't you lighten the load to help recover mentally?** Your mental health is just as important as your physical. And if you don't know how to deal with that mental load, that is what therapy is for. Peer support helps. CISM helps.

But if you have been dealing with an issue for more than a month. You can't let go. It keeps recycling in your brain. You dream about it. You avoid certain places if you can help it. The things you used to enjoy doing aren't fun anymore. The job is no longer a passion, but a burden. Maybe it's time, right?

Some law enforcement agencies are bargaining for a mental health day, so their members have an opportunity to have a mental health checkup every year. The evidence is pretty clear. As first responders we have an extra burden to carry compared to the general population. Take that opportunity provided to you through your EAP and unload some of your burden.

Start enjoying life a bit more.

<u>You</u> are worth it.

<u>Tuesday, May 9</u>

Tuesday here at WCPR. Thought I would wait a couple days before writing. Get a sense for what issues I'm having. The clients have their own demons to work on. I can't really spend too much energy on them. I was told I would still be a client partially. Somewhere in the 75% range. Probably an accurate portrayal. A lot of the educational stuff I missed because of my brain being squeezed to death in December.

So, what's been bugging me so far? Well, this afternoon someone at a nearby ranch shot a shotgun. I had a startle response. Not much of one, but it's still there. Damn it!

Then, this afternoon during a lecture on the body's response to a stressor, there was mention of the impact on speech. Which got me thinking back to the incident. **When did I have a hard time talking?** It was before I saw Pat, by several, several minutes. It was actually after Greg told me about the burn-over.

I listened to the tapes. **I was stammering. Couldn't talk right.** And maybe that is why I used the radio identifier on the air? Maybe. It could also account for **why I don't remember how long I sat there in front of Jim's house.** I don't remember the dozer transport pulling up next to me, until the air brakes released. Hell, I hardly recognized John Jessen when he approached the truck. So what was the <u>actual</u> CI (critical incident)? Now I'm not sure. Something to discuss with the doc next week.

Another issue that was a bit of a trigger. Sunday started with a **discussion on suicide. I felt unsettled. Didn't sleep worth shit that night**. Carried over into the next day, Monday. Today, Tuesday, we watched the Code 9 video (trailer). Which I do remember from December. During this afternoon's debrief with the peers I was honest and said it was unsettling. Maybe because of a recent 1st Responder suicide in my county. I'm sure that's part of it. But maybe it's because I realize more and more that maybe I was getting to the end of my rope in December.

If I had had to wait until May 21 of this year (my originally scheduled date to attend) I don't know how I would have fared. Not that it matters. Wilson offered up his seat for me. And I am so glad he got to go to Arizona last week. I can hardly wait to talk with him. Also glad Duck got in last session. Definitely want to have lunch with him next week.

What else is bugging me so far? Oh - **administrative betrayal.** I thought I was farther along that forgiving pathway, but obviously, while I was talking with Paget today, **that shit still has got my goat. Maybe that's why I'm coloring a fucking wart hog.** No idea.

I could also be a bit riled up because one of the peers, in his own

way, is trying to figure out what my issues are. **I sometimes don't want to talk about it**. But maybe talking about it helped me connect the dots to my first knowledge of the burn-over.

Another thing to think about, because some of the clients have talked about some early life sexual issues. Got me to remember my college roommate's rape. And that maybe ties into my issues with Curt.

Damn!!! I hate connecting fucking dots!!!

Anyhow, I've been pulling a lot of weeds since I've been here. Very therapeutic. Coloring is another version of healthy response mode. But it's brainless so more like meditation. Calms the mind.

Totally opposite of what this journaling session is doing for you, Linda. **As you are well aware, your left brain is on fire right now. And WTF is going on with your tooth? You had a fucking root canal on it!!** I'm not buying that it is still healing. It's got to be a stress response. Because it really flared today!

Ok, enough dots and coloring for today.

As Bob Newhart would say…

STOP IT!!!!!

[MADTV, 2001]

Wednesday, May 31

Just challenged Diane about her brain fog. Like "when are you going to get serious about your brain fog?!" text message to her accompanied by a picture of her glasses next to what I assume to be her morning dose of supplements. She's in court so I may not hear from her for a while. **Am I being too pushy** by also putting a spare copy of Dr. Amen's book <u>The Brain Warrior's Way</u> by her suitcase?

I think not. I was going to give that to her for her birthday back in 2016, only **my PTSD had me in such a hole, it didn't happen.**

I just can't sit idly by and watch that happen anymore.

<u>**Wednesday, June 14**</u>

Today's shitty first draft (SFD)

A term used by Brene' Brown

I have talked about this, done a FB live about it. But I haven't journaled about it. What is IT?

The Formula

The Rating Formula

A bunch of numbers that quantify, in black and white, **just how messed up I am** as a result of my Post-Traumatic Stress Injury. What was the number?

26% Whole Person Impairment.

That is not the baseline number though.

That 26% is the number that has been adjusted, multiple times.

- For age.
- For occupation.
- For the psychological injury itself.

A whole bunch of insurance jargon that comes out to the final determination of just how fucked up you really are.

How fucked up <u>I</u> really am.

And that is mood-altering number.

Stunning, and not in a good way.

I spoke my truth.

And the insurance industry spit out a number.

Apparently, the journaling gods have determined that I don't need to obsess about it this morning beyond what I have already written.

Bottom line, and there is a bottom line.

I'm not going to get any worse, unless I start drinking again. I've already had that conversation with myself.

"To drink is to die." Done.

**How much I improve is totally dependent on my actions and intentions, determined on a daily basis.**

I meditate to calm my anxiety, to recognize early on when something is "off" in my body.

I journal to figure things out. To acknowledge pain points. To discover options to learn that in many cases, I already had the answer.

SUMMARY – 2ⁿᵈ Quarter 2017

New year. New therapist. The transfer of care took more time than I cared for, but it was out of my control. The month of January my primary focus was on sleep. No longer driven by the need to get to work, I turned off all alarms, and told my husband to just let me sleep. After nearly three weeks of nine or more hours of sleep each night, I started to feel somewhat normal.

My journaling practice became more sporadic, but the self-examination deepened. I changed my post-therapy routine. Instead of rocking out in my truck on the drive home, I stopped at the local coffee shop and treated myself to a double dark chocolate mocha while I journaled about our discussion. It sucked sometimes, but the insights I gained were priceless.

My first trip back to the retreat, this time as a peer, was emotionally painful. I was still raw in many ways. Due to the change in therapists at the turn of the new year, I had done little mental work since I retired. I was very flat emotionally. The trip back gave me perspective though. Most of the peers there in May had also been there in December 2016 when I went through. A discussion on medications opened me up to considering them as my next best step in recovery.

The insurance numbers game would continue to play out well into 2018. A review of my case by a qualified medical examiner (QME) took into consideration what my life was like post-retirement, recognized the major depression I was now suffering from, and modified my permanent and stationary date. The bottom line? I'm more messed up than I originally thought.

By the end of June, with anti-depressants newly added to my daily routine, life seemed to be improving. For the first time in a couple of years, I almost felt "normal".

THIRD QUARTER: JULY - SEPTEMBER

Wednesday, August 16

Met with the nutritionist today.

Tofu?

If I feel the need to snack, have 2-3 options, and stick to them.

Have a diversionary tactic in mind, like 10 pushups or something active

Strive for consistency.

Thursday, September 7

It's been three weeks since last visit with the good doc.

Eating – okay

Sleep – okay

Sex – 0

So she talked about it.

Of course, she did.

Talked about a book, about women's sexual drive. The transition.

Impact on husband of **zero sex drive** is almost as stressful. Maybe even equal to the stress of watching me suffer.

Sooooo, my homework is to talk with Curtis about it.

Friday, September 8

While checking my email this afternoon, saw an email from Alan Knopp, point of contact for the LNU Retirees.

Announcing the death of Bryon Beck!!

He hadn't retired yet!!!

Last time I saw him was when we met for coffee at Studebakers in February.

He was delivering my retirement gift to me.

It was a great talk!

He was so happy!

I'm just stunned now.

NUMB

Monday, September 11

I remembered a dream this morning with Diane and Salina in the background.

I was helping Diane fold clothes (or maybe pack?) a pair of pants, conservative gray tweed, on the backside.

So I rotated them to fold along the front crease.

Hammer time! (as I remembered America's Got Talent tv show, with the Singing Trump act)

The front was lined with baby blue satin and white ruffles.

There was laughter.

My alarm sounded.

Wednesday, September 13

Told the good doc about my dream with the clown pants.

She thought some interesting things. Along the lines of my feminine *self*, trying to be aligned with the masculine uniform of work.

Her recommendation, crazy as it is…

a)   Share dream with WCPR folks, see what they think

b)   Take a pair of uniform pants and add some trim to one side only

c)   Maybe a shadow box showing the conflict

She practically started crying, something in my subconscious is coming awake, and that is a good thing.

(apparently, she has been able to interpret dreams since childhood)

She asked what Diane did for work [foster kids, adoptions]

Children <u>abandoned</u>

So part of my pain was the impact on the <u>children</u> of the fire

The destruction

Loss of "safe place"

Disruption

The iconic picture "girl with a doll"

Pictures of burned tricycles

The play structures at the pre-school

Is that why I was so drawn back to the place?

Ask the question.

So my pain was being felt by my feminine side. The masculine side was fighting the fire. The feminine side was coordinating the evacuations. Interesting perspective.

The role of Mama Green.

Reconciliation.

<u>Monday, September 18</u>

To my health.

Why?

Why did I **binge** today?

What possessed me to buy two bags of cookies? One on the premise that I would take it to the meeting.

So why 2 then?

Because I wanted the mint!

Yes, I know, no different than having that fucking drink!

I am so disappointed in myself! Is this where the negative self-talk kicks in? Sure seems like it!

Yes, just say it and move on.

FUCK IT! FUCK IT! FUCK IT!

Okay, so what is the source?

Curt's eye surgery? Why couldn't the doctor get <u>all</u> of the cataract? This is such an energy suck!

You just coached Jenn on this very thing! **Are you a fake? A phony? An imposter? Like WTF!!??**

It's going to take hard work to achieve this next thing. Right? You could just fold in the towel. Be forgotten within a few months. For what? I've been fighting my way back for what? The retirement home? I don't want that! I want to make a difference. I've been playing small, even before my injury. Selfish. Ah, that good old-fashioned alcoholic brain. Is that it? What is God's will in all of this? When is the last time you asked? Earnestly? For a month solid? It took 8 months to get that insight into Parkes. And all of this is what <u>you</u> want. Is your intention pure enough? Ask God about that. Do I have the right team? Ask God. **Am I enough?** Definitely, <u>ask</u> God. Eventually you will be provided an answer. The only way to find out though is to ask God in prayer.

<u>Friday, September 22</u>

Just meditated to "Letting Go of the Past & Being Free", guided 12-minute meditation. (Insight Timer app)

So how did that feel?

Peaceful   Quieting

Relaxing   Restful

Could feel the chi in my hands about halfway through.

No distressing thoughts.

The dogs barking outside.

Me not caring about that.

Shoulder muscles relaxing.

Letting go.

Summary – 3rd Q 2017

The yin/yang of life, neatly bundled into three months of my life.

On the one hand, trying to get my act together around the various areas of my physical health: weight management, sex life, exercise. On the other hand, radical self-doubt and hatred relative to my addictions: alcohol and sugar.

Two years since the fire, and no mention of it in any journal entry I have found yet. But those clown pants! Coming to grips that, as a retiree, I would find out about deaths and such through the inefficiencies of email and Facebook posts.

If this quarter had an undercurrent of a theme, it would be the reintegration of self.

I was beginning to *feel* again, as uncomfortable as it was.

FOURTH QUARTER: OCTOBER - DECEMBER

Thursday, October 26

What the hell just happened?

Well, it's like this. The wind blew. Many, many fires started within LNU/MEU. At night. Within 90 minutes of each other.

"Broken Arrow"

From Calistoga to Santa Rosa in 4 hours. Yes. 4 hours.

That was just the Tubbs fire.

Overall, the death toll will exceed 50, if not 75 by the time the "missing" stay that way forever.

5700 structures destroyed.

Homeless by the 1000's.

Untold lives destroyed!

But, it's not my trauma.

Friday, October 27

Friday. Interesting enough, my first day at the Peer Support trailer was Friday the 13th. My, how time flies. So here it is two weeks later. Still can't find a decent pen. My good one has disappeared into the bowels of the truck. **Yesterday I shared that I was numb.** For the most part, this feeling reminds me of that 18-month old boy we did CPR on in San Joaquin. As the paramedics were discussing clinically the various means of starting an IV on the child we all knew was dead. Not sure if surreal is the right word then, or now. I could so

relate to some of the things that were said in the trailer yesterday at the debrief. I did what I could to validate their feelings. Because that's how I felt after Cobb burned.

Familiar landmarks – gone.

Community – gone.

That sense of safety – GONE!

Late morning…

My writing practice has tailed off recently. And that's too bad. I find it to be cathartic in some ways.

Sat through the sales pitch at Wyndham just now. **Part of my brain was clicking along, doing the math. Another part felt pretty fucking clueless.** Although I remember the gist of the conversation in San Diego, the last time we upgraded, I don't remember the nuances. And **I used to be able to remember things like that.** So the more I engage with the real world, the more I realize what my "dis"ability is. **I used to have a mind like a steel trap.** Is it a natural part of aging, as suggested by the doctor? No, I don't think so. **Those "gaps" are becoming very noticeable the more I try to engage at the "old" speed of thinking on my feet.** The more I try to recall important things I learned such as the training on *Don't Be Phish Bait*. I remembered it, but <u>after</u> the damage was done.

Two years of my life that I only have vague memories of outside of the circle of pain from the PTSD. So, how do I cope with these gaps? How do I adjust?

I write more. That helps me retain information better. I shy away from situations that require instant decision making. I do not engage with life/death decisions. I can't do that again.

Drinking alcohol. I don't do that anymore because I <u>know</u> that to drink is to die. And the thought occurred to me the other day that I need to take that same stance with junk food and other unhealthy dietary choices. Right? I can Snicker bar my way to a 6-way emergency bypass, or I can <u>BE</u> healthy.

I AM.

I am here <u>now</u>.

I AM.

I AM HEALTHY.

I AM.

<u>I AM</u> is <u>BEING</u> this AT THIS TIME

IN THE PRESENT MOMENT.

I AM HEALTHY.

Say it out loud.

Again.

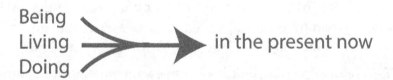

Today.

This 24 hours.

This moment.

This decision point.

<u>I AM HEALTHY</u>

And so I AM.

And so I AM.

<u>Tuesday, November 7</u>

What is going on? Clay wants me to envision being on stage constantly. So what trigger do I set? Let me sleep on it.

What is bugging you though? What is bugging <u>me</u>? **I feel boxed in.** Poised ready to strike. But boxed in. What am I doing? How do I level up when I **feel trapped?** Almost dismissed.

Doctor, I have **headaches**.

Oh, go get a massage.

Doctor, I feel like I'm having a **hard time recalling words**, etc.

Oh, maybe you're getting older.

Is it time to move on?

The 80/20 rule? 90/10?

90% of the effort will go into the last 10% of the work to be done?

Motivation is lagging.

Hooked on sugar.

Focus is toast.

Are these self-limiting beliefs?

I have no idea.

So let me ask my SELF this? Am I holding myself back? Going through the motions? What am I telling myself?

Have I been applying the GID? Tools?

Honestly? No.

<u>Journal every day?</u> Not even close.

<u>Gratitude – every day?</u> Uh, no!

<u>Prayer and Meditation?</u> This is part of your recovery for both PTSD and AA.

Has to be.

HAS TO BE!

Journaling – practically writes the book.

What about REDEMPTION as a theme? Are you even bitter, just a touch, after reading the article about 1st Responder resiliency?

What does that feel like?

Numb – are you just saying that, so you don't have to answer? Like today on the call. Circular reasoning. I feel nothing.

So I'm okay. I'm "FINE"
- **Fouled up**
- **Insecure**
- **Neurotic**
- **Emotional**

Resiliency, as part of a "social" process.

Resiliency, as a core competency.

Resiliency, as a model that includes asking for help, for <u>mental health.</u>

Ponder that.

Wednesday, November 15

Here I am at WCPR, interesting discussions.

I am worthy of <u>respect.</u>

Multiple discussions with peers regarding my interactions with the chief. So, what are the facts?

Not feelings or emotions.

Plenty of facts…

… trying to figure out if there's enough for an EEO claim.

Why does this have power over me? Relates to 4th Step – what lies under/behind the fear? What is/was the common theme?

Abandonment.

He didn't take care of me when I was most vulnerable.

Connect the dots…

"I'm not good enough."

Dates back to when I about 5 years old. Got my first bike that year, with training wheels, on my birthday in February. Sometime in May it was discussed about removing the training wheels. I was circling the yard, demonstrating to Dad that I was a good rider. One of the training wheels got caught in the edge of the lawn, and down I went. Dad said I wasn't good enough <u>yet</u>. I jumped back on my bike to prove that I was.

This insight provided by a 45-minute meditation session.

Thursday, November 16

About 4 am. I woke up, not suddenly, but noticed that I was damp with sweat. Would rate that a C- for a **night terror**.

Later in the day…

The retreat is almost over. This one went well. I feel better about my involvement.

So what did I learn about myself this week?

"I'm not good enough" is a script written 50 years ago.

Yes. Five Zero years.

Love you Dad, but… (sarcasm dripping here) thanks for the vote of confidence – NOT!

A reminder that forgiving does not mean <u>condoning</u> behavior.

Report the facts. Let someone else judge.

Wednesday, November 22

About that dream last night.

A blend between old and new?

I was in a class with other students. We had an art project to work on, with an upcoming deadline. Some sort of drawing with an overlay of machine-cut lettering. Only one machine, in another building. Outside the art building, an old road with a barricade at the end. On the other side was a dry weed-free ditch, which extended straight out for at least 100 yards.

Between the two buildings (sunny day, green grass – like a school quad) some dude shows up, asking where he can find a hill to practice a hose lay. He's in civilian clothes, long shaggy blonde hair. Has a hose and nozzle in his hands. He had just walked in from the direction of the ditch.

Someone said we don't do that around here, and someone stopped to talk with him.

Meanwhile, back at the machine shop, the other students had their stuff done, and it was finally my turn. Other students asked if I needed help, and I said yeah. Go back to the other classroom and clear a space for my background piece, and as soon as I get this cut, I can hustle back and put it in place before the deadline. Typical chaos surrounding a deadline, but I got it done.

Back on Sunday I was working on a video presentation (draft) and I wanted to make a point visually. So I walked over to my closet where my uniform shirt has hung since sometime in the spring. (Yes, it took me that long to pick it up from where I had thrown it last December after my last day at work.)

Anyhow, I took the badge off the shirt to show it to the camera. That is the first time I've had it in my hands since I retired.

Monday, November 27

I can't afford to absorb any other people's negativity with my PTSD. I have expended a tremendous amount of energy crawling out of the "pit of misery". I will not be the crab being dragged back into the crab pot.

What demands respect?

That is an age-old question.

Is it wisdom, beauty, or grace?

Or something else?

What action, prose, or face?

Calls for the question?

Is it speed, brains, knowledge, skills, abilities?

Common sense, or rank?

Why do we pay respect?

And what is the currency?

Where lies the value of respect?

If demanded, what is the price?

Of that give and take?

What rent is paid like a common tenant?

Once given, as demanded, it's gone forever

as worthless as a 3-dollar bill.

Once offered, as a gift, it lingers softly

A priceless gossamer feather.

So, respect has a currency

Intangible

Sightless

Aura of being

Two people, side by side

Both with respect, no doubt

Who is the better?

The Gift, Freely Given

The Gossamer Feather

Wednesday, November 29

Voice message from the QME doctor. Having a medical procedure, will be out for at least 90 days. The QME is cancelled. SCIF will be notified.

Now I have to deal with that all over again.

Wednesday, December 6

In Concord area at the Amen Clinic.

[brain fog...lack of focus...motivation] enough already! FIX IT!

The Intake Process

I like that I could download and print the basic paperwork, to read at my leisure and sign ahead of time.

Met with Simone, lovely lady. She will be my case manager. Reviewed my 17-page intake electronic questionnaire.

Count backwards from 100, by 7

Back to the waiting room. Filled out two paper brain function

questionnaires.

The Scan Process

Start IV port. Tech explained the process. "Don't click X" during test. Got a 30-second practice test. Oh Hey! The speed changes.

The real thing is about 14 minutes long. About 2/3 of the way through the tech came back in to administer the radioisotope solution. I didn't even notice that she pulled out the IV port.

The scan itself. About 20 minutes long. The frame rotates around. Brushes against shoulder. Cozy fit. Grateful for the warm sheet and blanket, pillow under my knees.

My head was held in place by a strap around my forehead. My head itched after I was moved into the tube. (Of course, it did!)

While in there I remembered the deer accident from work. Another headache.

During the scan I had one of those **whole-body tics**. Haven't had one like that for a while.

Anyhow, it's a step forward.

Tomorrow, scan #2, Resting.

Thursday, December 7

Scan #2.

Again, no caffeine.

Stayed in truck listening to 80's rock until 5 minutes before appointment. David Bowie – China Girl.

Taken into a different room, with a recliner. This is supposed to be the "quiet brain" scan. Took two attempts to get the IV started in the right arm. But now I know a decent vein exists on the lower biceps area. Not in the crook of the elbow.

The technician left me to quiet my mind. Then she came in and shot the nuclear soup and removed the IV. Less than a minute? Left quietly, so I just chilled for several more minutes. Then straight to the scan tube, warm blanket and all. 20 minutes. Chill out. Not thinking of anything complex. Actually, a nice quiet mind meditation.

Tomorrow, meet with Dr. Emina to review the results.

Stand by to stand by…

Wednesday, December 20

My morning muse…

My brain is somewhat in a spin cycle. So much information delivered since the beginning of the month. The brain scan and results. Hell, even the results I have noticed since starting on the supplements. Who knew that specific exercises benefitted different parts of the brain? Dr. Amen even has a brain study course, including a discussion on supplementation. Add that to my 2018 agenda. Yes.

And the Firehouse Expo has several breakouts on mental health. I need to be there. Mingle. Start figuring out how to get there someday before I'm 60.

What measurable goals or events? What results? How to say it in such a way that makes sense? Okay, **you're trying to think too hard this morning. That's why there is a blockage.** The goal of your morning muse is to dump out that crap so you can function better throughout the day. And so that is all I'm going to say about the puzzle for now.

So, what else is on my mind? My goal is long-term sobriety because I know going back will kill me. And that is **suicide by bottle.** So, there it is there.

My life is worth living. Because I have contributed enough recently to other PTSD sufferers (and their spouses) that I have felt how that feels. Finally.

And I want to thank Clay for helping me find that emotional point, that good hit of dopamine. BrainGeekRUs. Ha ha ha. Love it!

Really !!

I'm smiling right now. Because I am!

Later on, appointment with the good doc…

What's still open for discussion?

Moving forward, to unburden myself. Forgive does not mean condone.

Still dealing with brain injury to pre-frontal cortex. Impaired ability to rationalize. Will you burn bridges? Yes. Does it matter? No. Why not? How many of your "friends" have called you in the last year? Other than Junior? That would be zero, zip, nada, zilch. Big fat goose egg. 0. So why should it matter then? You planning on returning to work? No, I don't need the pressure. So let it be. Let go.

It's unfinished business. Finish it.

The old ways no longer serve you.

Summary – 4th Quarter 2017

I ventured out of my comfort zone and dipped my toes back into the world of chaos. The fires were so widespread and destructive they demanded my attention. Earlier in the year I had received training to participate on critical incident stress teams, and it was time to see how I would (or could) function in that role. As long as I stayed out of the smoke, I was good. Eventually, I ventured out to the fire area, and met people where they were. We both benefitted from the experience.

I also became painfully aware of the gaps in information recall that my brain was dealing with. **For the second time in three months, I was scammed, and my bank account was compromised. The long-term implication of that lack of function was downright scary as hell.** What would life be like in the future if I couldn't protect myself from the jackals of the world?

My fear drove me to action. I had been at a couple of conferences where Dr. Daniel Amen had discussed brain health. The first time, I was more concerned about dementia because of Mom's last years. The second time I heard him speak, I interjected my own brain health into the conversation. As a result, I picked up the 500-pound phone and scheduled myself for a SPECT scan. I was fortunate to have the financial resources to pay out-of-pocket for it, and the subsequent blood work, without trying to convince worker's comp or my own health provider of the need.

Just as being diagnosed with PTS brought some relief, knowing I wasn't going crazy, the scan results also brought relief. Yes, part of my **pre-frontal cortex was off-line** when it should have been engaged with the computer task, and my **basal ganglia was lit up like a Christmas tree** when it should have been "chilling" with me. Over the next few months, I worked with the psychiatrist to optimize my prescription medications, and to build up a supplement routine that would support me and my brain.

It took me a couple of weeks to start noticing the difference. My husband noticed the difference within two days.

Unfortunately, insurance companies take the cheapest route possible to assist people with PTS. Everything, even EMDR, has to be requested and approved before treatment can be provided. The odds of my worker's compensation system approving a SPECT scan was slim, and none. It wasn't cheap, but by then my belief in my self-worth had been bolstered by the treatment I was getting.

SECTION 5

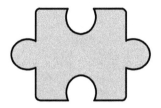

RETURN TO CENTER

2018

FINDING MY NEW NORMAL

Breaking out of the rut of the previous three years was going to take a massive shift in energy. I wasn't sure how I was going to accomplish this "shift". I knew, though, that it needed to happen, and all the therapy and retreat time wasn't enough to make it happen. It was time for me to generate some energy into living life to my fullest. Otherwise, what was the point of recovering?

I asked my husband what he wanted to do to celebrate our upcoming wedding anniversary.

"A weekend at the coast would be nice" was his response.

I tapped the fingers of one hand into the palm of my other hand and called for a timeout. "Allow me to rephrase the question. It will be our 30th wedding anniversary. Our passports are collecting dust. Where would you like to go to celebrate our anniversary?"

"Scotland" was his first response. In short order he added Ireland. After a few minutes he offered Australia as an option, because that has been on my bucket list for over a decade.

"It's not about me, it's about us, and your first choice was Scotland, so that is where we will go." Our first ever solo international trip seemed like a good idea, and an adventure worth happening. I had roots there, so I was intrigued to see the land my ancestors had come from. Besides, as an island, there would be plenty of coast line to visit.

Our first challenge quickly raised its hand and said "Um, excuse me? Do you even *know* where your passports are?" A minor detail to be sure. However, without a passport, you can't book international flights. Some silly rule, but it was a challenge to be dealt with. Three days later, the mystery was solved, and we could proceed with trip planning.

I added in a layover in Pennsylvania, so we could visit family. It is significantly easier for the two of us to visit the grandkids, then it is for Curt's daughter, my step-daughter, to load up her large family and travel to California.

So one fine day in April, we found ourselves surrounded by nearly 20 children, dogs, and puppies. It was chaotic, and fun, all wrapped up into one massive bundle of energy. Aided, in part, by the coffee bar conveniently located in the dining room. I'm not talking about a Mr. Coffee or a Keurig machine. Melissa has _the_ Cuisinart Coffee Center, and the Torani syrup, and everything else.

A few days later we bid adieu, properly fortified by massive amounts of love, puppy breath, (and coffee), and boarded our British Airways flight to London.

Heathrow Airport is not a small place. With five major terminals, let's just say it is spread out. We might have missed our connecting flight to Inverness if not for a Customer Service representative who guided us through the maze, got us to the front of the line in Customs, and figured out what gate we needed to be at to get to Inverness.

Twenty minutes later, we were in the air. With a window seat, I was able to look at the lay of the land. The greenness of the hillsides. Snow-topped mountains. The openness of it all. The stress of the previous few days started to wear off. The stress of the previous two years started to lose its grip.

At least, it all seemed good until we picked up the rental car. The rental car, with the steering wheel on the right side, because they drive on the left side of the street in Scotland. Did I mention it was a manual transmission? And they have these things called round-abouts instead of controlled intersections. For what it's worth, it was also rush hour, such as it is, in Inverness. And my jetlagged body was screaming for a nap.

I will say, though, their onboard GPS system is superb compared to what is available here in the states. We eventually found our cozy AirBnB and settled in for a short nap before dinner. A nearby pub offered a dinner menu, and we walked over to stretch our legs. The cook had left early that day, so we had to settle for what we could find at the neighborhood mini-mart.

And so began our two week adventure in Scotland. We would eventually sail on Loch Ness, explore the Scottish coast, climb through castles, eat haggis, and be told we had beautiful American accents. We even figured out how to put the car in reverse. I found the abbey, what was left of it, where my great (x8) grandfather had been baptized in the 1700's before leaving for America as a child.

We witnessed the ingenuity of the Scottish people at the Falkirk Wheel and marveled at the scale and the creativity of the Kelpies. By design, we ended our trip in Gourock, to attend the Scottish Games. Part county fair, part competition, part celebration of all things Scottish, we immersed ourselves into the culture, asked questions, took pictures, and relaxed.

At the end of that glorious spring day, as I put my camera away, I realized I felt different. It was subtle but it was significant and very real. I felt happy. Satisfied. Content. I traveled half way around the world to find myself and be whole again.

NEW FIRE

In late July 2018, the River Fire started near Hopland. The smoke was blown into my neighborhood by the prevailing west winds. The heavy smoke in the air put me on edge, which did not surprise me because that is a known trigger to me.

At the time, one of our granddaughters was visiting us. With her help, we had emptied out the entire garage so that we could paint the walls and the ceiling. We had pulled everything out so that we could organize it and turn part of it into the rock shop so Curt could work on some of our hobby stuff.

We were in the process of putting things back in. The ash fall was noticeable, and we threw a tarp over our belongings still sitting on the front lawn. The fire was making a pretty good run pushed by the wind, and by the second day was within four miles of town. An evacuation advisory was issued for our neighborhood. We started loading up one of our vehicles with some valuables.

I'd already been restless for two days because of the smoke so the evacuation advisory just put me over the edge. My self-care routine had been disrupted, so I really had no clue that my anxiety was going on as strong as it was. I think it was a deeper seeded trigger than I originally thought. Between the smoke, young people, and the pace that the family was working, it took me back to when I was in Hobergs. And when I was thinking that people were moving too slow and they basically needed to get the fuck out right now so that's where I was, but I didn't realize I was there. Looking back on it, I can see clearly now that **I was in the midst of a flashback.** In the moment though, I was consumed by it.

I abruptly told my husband that both he and our granddaughter needed to get moving. They just needed to leave, and my brother and I would do what we could around the house and finish securing it as best we could. Then we would follow up with the dogs.

Somewhere along the line there was even more miscommunication. He thought I would be on the road within the next hour or so. That wasn't _my_ thought process. Pretty much, I didn't have a thought process. I was triggered, and I was just reacting and trying to secure the house.

Oddly enough, as many evacuation orders that I had ordered or had rolled into a fire with evacuations already in place, I had never been on the receiving end of an evacuation order. That added stress and because it was my home, it was much more personal. I was trying to get things done around the house and put at least more valuable things back into the garage like our tools. Or, I was cutting back weeds. Or, moving the propane tanks into the back yard where they might be sheltered from the fire. As long as I was moving, I was functioning.

My brother and I worked until about six o'clock that evening. The fire officials hadn't changed the evacuation order at all. It was still at the advisory level, so we decided to spend the night at the house and reconsider in the morning. The dogs were relaxed. I was feeling a bit better. We were watching baseball on TV later in the evening, when my brother received a phone call. He left the room to talk.

He came back downstairs after the call and informed me that my husband was really mad that we weren't already on the road. He implied there might be some ramifications behind that, so I called my husband. No doubt about it, he was mad. I assured him we would be on the road in the morning.

In the morning, we finished picking up stuff around the house, and cutting back a few more weeds. Both of our vehicles were loaded. We grabbed the dogs and left. My dog Schatze gets all worked up whenever we go for a ride. Excessively so this day. Within an hour, I had to stop and clean up the back seat. By the time we got to Williams the evacuation order had been raised to mandatory.

The whole time I was driving I was trying to think what had happened, why had it happened that way? Why had I acted the way I did yesterday? The only thing I could come up with was I had been triggered. I just didn't realize it in the moment. Between the heavy smoke, the urgency, and the pace of people I was triggered. Prior to having a post-traumatic stress injury those things would not have bothered me at all. I would have just gone about my business. I could have tapped into my stubborn nature and say, "Hey, unless and until they make it mandatory, we're going to stay here".

That's not what happened though. My brain said, "Hey, there's heavy smoke in the air, and there's family at risk, and there's a child at risk", which is also a real heavy trigger for me. My fight, flight or freeze response really kicked in, and I had ordered my husband to leave several hours before he really needed to.

Once I arrived where he was staying, and got the dogs settled in, we sat down for a discussion. It was not a comfortable conversation to have, but I had to apologize for treating him as I had. To be clear, I did not apologize for the trigger. I didn't use it as an excuse for my behavior either. Meditation helps me contain my anxiety, and I had not been consistent with my practice the previous few weeks. That fact I own totally.

Again, sometimes triggers are hidden. You think you know all of them and how they impact you. However, there are still some sneaky little devils out there and they pop up every now and then.

RANDOMNESS

For example, just last week I was scrolling through my Instagram account. I follow a wide variety of sites such watercolor painting, personal development, and dogs. I still follow some firefighting sites because, as a former firefighter, I still like watching things, and it helps me gauge if I'm being triggered by something that I may not know about. Such was the case here.

There was a demonstration of two young firefighters racing each other to put on all of their structure gear and throw on a breathing apparatus. Something happened during the course of that video, maybe my energy was low to begin with, I don't know. However, I quickly and harshly critiqued their efforts without taking into consideration that maybe they were just doing a quick demonstration because some children were visiting the firehouse. I didn't take into consideration that maybe they already agreed not to go "on air".

That video has been viewed over 50,000 times and it's been interesting reading some of the comments that were posted in response to my comments. I shouldn't be upset by the five comments kicked

back at me, but I had been ruminating about them for three or four days. I talked with someone I trusted about the whole situation. He asked me what I thought about the people that made those negative comments?

"Well, they're morons" I said.

"If you're thinking that they're morons, what's that say about you?"

"Okay, I'm a moron, because I made those comments to begin with…" which got me laughing. That kept me from responding to some of the comments that had come in. I figured out how to delete the comment because it wasn't helping anyone, me in particular.

Some of the comments were really interesting though. One person said, "Hey, you know, you must be a nightmare to work with". I have my moments and I think everybody does, but I wasn't all that upset by that one. Then there was the comment implying my lack of professionalism. Again, we all have bad days. I just happened to have it on a very public forum. Another person actually expressed a little concern, and suggested I take a break from social media. I actually appreciated that gentleman's comment.

There is one that really came across as completely out of line and I just have to address it. I hope this person doesn't treat the women in his life this way when they're having a bad day. The commentator told me to go get a "good fuck and have a stiff drink". Really, is that what we tell everybody who is having a bad day? Just go get a good fuck?

I don't know if that is stigma against PTSD, or stigma against "uppity" women or whatever. Regardless, let's get real here people. People have bad days and people with PTSD also have bad days. Instead of coming across like a total jerk, offer up a little compassion.

Obviously, there is a trigger I need to work on. I've already reached out to my therapist to try and get in later this week. I continue to do the work that helps me regain my sense of humanity. I am hopeful that the person that railed against me does the same.

Triggers pop up every now and then. There is a transition to go from the generalized day-after-day suffering from post-traumatic stress, where anything and everything can trigger you, to just being in certain circumstances or situations where you see something on a video or in real life and just out of the blue, you get triggered. I don't think that's a negative thing. I think it's just a fact that you need to be aware of as you continue to live with post-traumatic stress. Realize that the long-term ramifications of PTS are that those sneaky little devil triggers are still out there.

You can be mad about that. "Damn! I thought was over this!!" I thought I had already worked on that trigger enough. Your brain keeps you honest though. If something pops up that you thought you're already done enough work on, it doesn't hurt you to go do another session about it.

Sometimes you don't know that something will trigger you until it does. The symptoms can be so mild that they get lost in the shuffle of everything else that was more extreme, that more urgently needed to be addressed. I still get subtle reminders that I still have some work to do and I accept that PTS has no cure. It is an injury that needs regular attention and healing.

DREAMS

I had a weird dream last night. I wasn't going to share it, because it was so upsetting to me. I realize now I've been sharing my story in this book, and you may have already been triggered by it. So here goes.

I was driving across a bridge and saw a school bus go nose first in the water, driven off the end of a ferry. And more cars were plunging in as I watched, helpless. I woke up and realized it was just a dream. I started to ruminate on it and figure out how the kids could enact their "miracle escape" from the sinking bus. I finally forced myself to get out of bed and get about my day.

Other than that, it's weird because I couldn't see how it had anything to do with my incident, or anything else for that matter. It was just a really negative dream. And I don't know… I have work to do with my therapist to interpret it. Anyhow, I thought I would just add another story so you know how, over the long-term, post-traumatic stress can show up.

Things pop up every now and then, whether it's something you thought you already dealt with, or it's a new thing. That's the way it is, and you can be mad about it, or you can just accept it and go work on it.

THE DREAM, AND WHAT IT IS ALL ABOUT…

It's all connected. You see, my dreams have never been about my "incident". My psyche is trying to communicate, to air out the serious discussion that needs to happen. When I finally met with my therapist a couple days later, we jumped right into the EMDR. We started with the gloveless hands from the video, connected the dots to not feeling prepared, which led to my viewpoint that the "kids" don't know what they don't know. My Phoenix trip was marked by a Mesa PD officer completing suicide. Four years on the job. An officer involved shooting. Loss of life. And the unsettling trend I had noticed that our officers, our firefighters, our paramedics, were completing suicide at a younger age.

At the retreat we teach that we don't necessarily choose the job. The job chooses us for a variety of reasons. We are attracted by the adrenaline, by the seeming ability to control a situation, by the camaraderie of the uniform. The academy is designed to teach the essential skills of the job. Experience will provide the rest of the knowledge needed to excel.

What we are not teaching the "kids" is how to survive the contrast between what we believe and what is actually happening. The moral code that says, "we save lives" versus "we can't save *all* lives" versus "sometimes you have to decide who you can save" versus "sometimes you have to take a life". These ethical dilemmas carry a heavy burden and when you enter a profession to "save" others, you also expect the department to "save" you. And that doesn't happen often enough.

The "dream" discussion led me to an image taken shortly after the Valley Fire of a little girl holding her doll, looking lost. I told the doctor that whenever and wherever I drove thru the wreckage of the fire, there were constant reminders of how lives, especially young lives, were being disrupted. Burnt bicycles in front yards. Singed trampolines in back yards. Pools filled with debris, turning green from algae. Which all seemed so overwhelming then.

This led to a discussion about this book. Will it really make a difference? While I have been pounding the keyboard, the suicide rate keeps climbing. Every day of delay adds another number, another name. How do I keep working in this venue when it seems impossible to make a difference?

Most days I wear a necklace with a fleur de lis charm. I was asked the other day what the fleur de lis means to me. "Hope", was my response. When I was at my lowest, I heard a story about hope, and that ignited a spark in me that carries me to this day.

As I thought about this dream for the week leading up to writing this section, I realized the hope I need to talk about doesn't just apply to the person out there suffering in their own mind. How do I help keep hope alive in the helpers of the world who literally and metaphorically walk into the fire to serve others? The doctors, the therapists, the chaplains, the peers? Family and friends? Random strangers who reach out a helping hand? It can be thankless work. How do people like that keep doing their stuff when the payoff may be years in the making, if they even get the chance to witness the win?

How do I keep hope alive in me?

While I was studying business, it was noted in a marketing class that every letter hand-written to a member of Congress represents the voice of a thousand people. What does that say about the power of a book? There's a stack of books next to me written by other First Responders who have suffered and struggled with Post-Traumatic Stress. Their voices represent tens of thousands of people who have

prevailed in their battle. The power of hope I gained from reading their stories carried me, lifted me up, and held space for me as I struggled. Their stories personify HOPE.

I don't have all the answers. I keep my own hope on an even keel by accepting that I can't save everyone. I surround myself with people who care about the world. I volunteer so I can see the faces of those I aim to help and celebrate their wins. So I can hear their laughter as they grab onto this message.

Their stories gave me a voice, and a choice.

I hope.

Therefore, I am.

SECTION 6

THE ROADMAP

YOUR GPS

THE TREE OF LIFE

Concept by Linda Green

THE ROADMAP

As I dive more into my creative side, I realize just how visual a person I am and so, as I worked on this book, I sometimes took a break from writing to sketch things out. While I was at the academy for a week-long class on fire behavior predictions, I sped through the modeling work related to fire spread rates and intensity using nomograms. One of the foresters teaching the class was amazed that I was done so soon. It was hard to explain, but I could see what the numbers were saying, even before the charts provided the answers.

I wanted a model to work from for this section. I had no idea what shape it would take. I just set up my easel and flipchart, grabbed a handful of pens, and drew my way through and into this concept of recovery. Part of it is based on my coaching certification, part is based on my interpretation of my own journey, and tools that I believe will help others with their own recovery process.

Everyone is unique. What worked for me may not work for someone else but I do believe though, that no stone can go unturned when you have a post-traumatic stress injury. I say this with great sincerity. There are thousands of different potential combinations of signs and symptoms, that affect hundreds of thousands of people. Some treatment protocols work reasonably well for some people. But not everyone. Some medicines work reasonably well for some people. But not everyone. That doesn't mean you don't try any of it.

It does mean that if the first thing you try doesn't work, you need to try something else. This is not a blank permission slip to go to therapy once or twice and say, "See!! Therapy didn't work for me! I tried it!" Or, to quit taking your anti-depressants because you feel better. Going to therapy and taking your medicine as directed is a commitment you make to yourself.

I swore to myself that I was willing to try and do anything and everything I could to beat this thing. There are some brilliant people out there who have been studying and working with people who have post-traumatic stress injuries for decades. I put some faith into

that system. I didn't want to go to therapy. I didn't want to take medicine. I had managed to muddle my way through life for decades with minimal outside interference.

So what changed, you ask?

I was fighting for my life...and that changed _everything_.

Are you ready to get to work now?

Awesome. Let's go.

THE TREE OF LIFE

I spent a lifetime in the forest. It is really no wonder that the concept that came to life that afternoon took the form of a tree. Three integrated parts that, when they are all in alignment, the tree thrives. And, three integrated parts that when the person is in alignment, the person thrives. When something is off, life can get a bit bumpy. When all three are off-kilter, life is hell. That is where post-traumatic stress takes us...to hell. Getting back to some semblance of normal requires awareness and a continuous effort of trial and error.

It helps when you have a reference point. Before I get into that, though, let me explain a bit more about this tree. The three parts, from top to bottom, are the crown, the trunk, and the roots.

The crown is living a vibrant and fulfilling life. On a more tangible side, it includes the body, mind, and spirit. The intangibles include healing, leaning in, triggers, and stinkin' thinkin'

What does this mean though? The essence of who we are lies in our deepest sense of self – the soul. And when we address the aspects of what is flourishing, it allows us to live a more vibrant life, thriving in our recovery.

If you consider the trunk to represent your spine, these elements allow you to move with the challenges of life. Your resiliency to the negatives in life. Like, ouch that hurt. A lot! But I am tougher than that. Is that the best you got?

'I AM' lives in the trunk. Courage lives here. The ability to stay true to your nature lives here. I am worthy. I matter. I am. I will. I can. Your ability to be calm in the face of adversity. The ability to be your own advocate. Mission for life. Acceptance of what is. They all live here.

The overall strength of the tree is the Root system. It is what connects us to greater world. It is what keeps us grounded. The people we have in our lives: Family, Friends, Co-workers, and Community.

Even our choice of career adds to this stability. The culture we allow ourselves to be in. Our own personal manifesto. Our underlying sense of WHY?

RETURN TO CENTER

Given this imagery of a tree as our recovery process, where then do we start? At the top and work our way down to the roots? Or do we start with the root system and work upwards from there? As wonky as this sounds, the reality is we need to start in the middle. YOU need to start in the middle. The trunk of the tree is your core. It is the essence of who you really, truly are when allowed to live freely without constraint. Who you really are in spite of the challenges you face.

Who you really are when it matters most.

The trunk is your inner courage, your resiliency, your faith. It holds together the things that make you, YOU. Your external environment plus your innermost beliefs and thoughts.

The trunk of the tree is your most powerful statement.

I AM

It says everything about you. That you are worthy. That you matter. That you are enough. Your drive. The essence of who you are that allows you to say

I Can

I Will

Because I AM

Where do we go from there? Isn't that enough? No, it's not. Post-traumatic stress injuries fragment our sense of self. We lose touch with the things we do to feel fully alive and vibrant. The things that we do as we live into the best version of our SELF. They matter too. The crown of the tree represents your actions. The things that you do intentionally to live the life of your choice.

For example, before my injury I saw myself as a physically fit person. With my PTS injury, I lost sight of that belief and vision of myself. My sleep was disrupted. I ate like crap. I drank way too much coffee and soda, not to mention alcohol. Not only did I lose sight of my vision, but my actions took me further away from my ideal. I gained weight. I became dehydrated. Sleep deprivation was the rule, not the exception.

Until I regained my sense of SELF enough to believe that I was worthy, that I was more than enough, to see that I AM is a choice, my choice, I couldn't take action on my vision. As my core sense of self came back into alignment, I could then start to take action on my vision of being physically fit.

I changed my sleep routine so I could get more than 3 hours of sleep. I drank more water and less caffeine. I quit alcohol for 90 days, and then committed to a year. I intentionally took action on my nutrition. I got my body moving again. Am I where I want to be on all those issues? Not even close. The message here though is that, until I re-established the belief in myself that I am worthy and that I matter, I couldn't move on those things that matter for my physical fitness. And if I couldn't take care of that which I value most, I couldn't be okay with myself.

My mind took a similar hit. I used to be an avid reader. I used to be able to remember the things that I read and apply them to my everyday life. That was part of my joy. One of the things I used to do to bring color into my life. The dysfunction of my brain took that away from me. Instead of practicing my 1000-yd stare, I exercised my mind too. I started to use coloring books. I did Sudoku puzzles. Played mahjong on the computer. Listened to Audible books. Yes, even watercolor painting helped

My brain eventually started to hit on more cylinders, more often. If I hadn't been doing those things, those brain exercises, this book could not happen. That trip to Scotland never would have happened without reconnecting with the belief that I AM is all the energy I need to start.

Alignment with your true self, with your pure essence of who you are and why you do the things you do with passion, is meaningless unless you also share all that you are with others. The people in your life mean something.

I'm not talking about the shallow relationships you may have with acquaintances where it's all about "Hi. Bye." Whether you are doing that to someone else, or that is being done to you, these

relationships don't impart meaning into our lives.

Try this experiment and note the difference. For two days, any-time you purchase something from a store, restaurant, coffee shop, or street vendor, don't make eye contact, no chit chat. Just pay your bill and move on. How did that make you feel? I'm pretty sure that impersonal exchange didn't make you feel warm and fuzzy or add to your "I feel really good about myself" factor. Now, how do you think that made the clerk feel? Especially if that is all they get from every interaction for an entire shift, day after day?

Now repeat the process, hopefully at the same places you just visited, and hopefully with the same sales clerks. This time, though, smile an honest-to-goodness smile. Use their name at least twice in the exchange. How about now? How did that make you feel? How do you think that made them feel?

Most people probably don't even have to conduct the experi-ment. They already know that a smile lights people up inside. They can feel the sound of music when they hear their name. If you don't have a clue what I'm talking about, then you really need to do this experiment.

The truth is, connections matter.

When you have post-traumatic stress, one of the early victims with your presence, or lack thereof, is with the connections in your life. As you shut down, as your amygdala sends false signals of mistrust and anger, the strength of your connections begins to erode. It's a subtle shift at first. You stop doing things that used to matter. You can't be "bothered" to go to your kids' school event. You no longer go fishing with your friends. Your spouse can't do anything right, no matter how hard they try.

Left unchecked, your PTS disconnects you from everything that brought joy and meaning into your life. When your cup is no longer being filled, you have nothing left inside to give from. You stop caring. You isolate. You think harshly, "They don't understand!!!" It's not that they don't or aren't capable of understanding. You are in pain, and it is hard to say that, even with your closest friends and family. Without even realizing it, you begin to slowly detach and isolate from the very connections that give you and your life purpose. That keep you grounded.

Connections feed the soul. They provide the color commentary (for you sports-minded people) to the narrative of our lives. Without them, we are just a shell of atoms floating through the cold vacuum of space.

What am I talking about when I speak of connections? Not so much what, but whom. Family and friends. Co-workers and peers. Your community. The culture you created that allowed you to thrive. The career that meant so much. That thing that used to get you out of bed each morning, excited for the day ahead. All of those are connections.

They matter.

They all matter.

Deeply.

The vibrancy of your crown, the alignment of your life, allows you to bend with the winds of life without breaking. Your trunk, your core essence, your character, holds you solidly on task as the debris of life bounces off your bark. And your connections? They

draw the nutrients from the soil, feed you, and sustain you.

Unfortunately, with PTS, as the brain, <u>your</u> brain, continues to misfire, and feeds you an excessive amount of stress hormones and chemicals, you start to wither and weaken as the onslaught of poison seeps ever deeper. It's a pretty dismal picture. Left unchecked, you lose everything.

If you're reading this though, I believe you are looking for a way to stem the flow, to turn the tide. It's not easy. But then again, all things in life worth fighting for, are not easy. You may have heard that before in your life. I just don't believe in sugar-coating the challenges that you will face while recovering from your Post-Traumatic Stress Injury. Not only is it going to suck, be prepared to likely feel worse before you feel better. I have to say this, because it is true.

It's messy work but it will get you unstuck and back to feeling more and more like yourself before your injury, so it's all worth it. You will feel frustrated. You will get angry. Oh wait, you already are. Right?

Okay, if you are ready to tackle what may be the biggest challenge you have ever faced, here's what I want you to do.

Get a journal you can write in. A cheap 50-cent composition book from the local dollar store will do just fine. Or spend the money and get something that looks good and makes you feel good. You deserve the best. Go for it!

Pick a time of day when you have about an hour of uninterrupted time. Make sure you have had something healthy to eat beforehand. Drink 8-12 ounces of water and have another glass of water by your side.

Listen to some music that won't distract you. I like listening to jazz when I'm studying. Find something that soothes you. If you're not sure, experiment.

This recovery "thing" is not something you can just pound through in a few hours and be done with it. I want you to take notes. I want you to write what something means to you, and why.

I want you to apply the things you learn.

I want you to find yourself again. The world needs you.

Ready?

Awesome!

Let's go!

I AM

Do you feel clear about who you are?

This is an important question, and you need to treat it with respect. As you answer it, treat yourself with respect also. Post-traumatic stress forces us away from our authentic self. The "real" us. The REAL you.

If you wear a uniform at work, whether as a member of the military or as member of the various colors of the "Thin Line", protecting citizens from the chaos of the world, I want you to put aside that uniform for now. This exercise is not about your work presence.

I want you to get to know you, as you are, at a core level. Who are you really, at the core and beneath all that bravado? Maybe it's been a while since you've spent any time alone with that person. Either the uniform or the PTS, maybe both, has moved you away from your center; your authentic self.

And if you think I am being all "woo-woo" here, I am not. I'm being a chief officer. I'm being a coach. I get paid to challenge peo-

ple, to help them improve and level up. I am challenging you, right here, right now, to go find your SELF again.

I'm not going to read your answers. You don't have to share them with anyone. Just be honest with yourself, okay?

Spend 15 minutes or so here and answer the question:

WHO are you?

A Life Well-Lived is Intentional

You just spent a bit of time reminding yourself of who you really are. If you don't like some of the answers, that's okay. I don't like everything about me either. I still have work to do. This isn't about perfection. As a human, I have flaws. We all do. We can certainly be hyper-critical of ourselves. That is really easy to do in the midst of PTS.

If you spent some time kicking yourself in the ass in the previous exercise, stop it. What you wrote out was just a snapshot in time. That was then. This is now. Stay focused on the NOW and FUTURE YOU.

Who are you when you are acting from the perspective of being your BEST self? What are you thinking? What actions show up?

Spend a few minutes here and write down the many ways you can show up as your BEST self.

My BEST Self

From the previous two exercises, pick 3 words that define the BEST of who you are. You will use these words to guide your <u>personal</u> life, including your thoughts and actions.

Word #1: _____

The reason I chose this word and why it's important to me...

Word #2: _____

The reason I chose this word and why it's important to me...

Word #3: _____

The reason I chose this word and why it's important to me...

Do This:

You have to remind yourself of your three words on a daily

basis. If you have a smart phone, set an alarm to go off at the same time each day. Use your three words as the label for the alarm. As an example, at 10:05 every morning, my alarm goes off, and my 3 words pop up on the screen. Every day I am reminded to be of service, live into my integrity, and exercise my creativity.

If you don't have a smart phone, write your three words on a 3x5 card, or a post-it note, or a scrap of paper. Hang it on your refrigerator, or bathroom mirror. Stick a copy in your wallet. Look at it every day, at the same time each day.

Want to Level UP?:

Say your three words out loud every day. Take pride in them. Embody them. Speak your truth. It's time to own who you truly are. Unapologetically.

COURAGE & CONTROL

CONFIDENCE

Confidence has several definitions, and includes concepts such as trust, self-assurance, certainty. All of which are eroded by PTS.

What I want to focus on right now though, is that feeling of self-assurance that arises from your appreciation of your own abilities or qualities. (New Oxford American Dictionary – online)

Another way to look at it comes from the Oxford American Writer's Thesaurus (online) that uses the example of "she's brimming with confidence", and includes such concepts as self-assurance, self-confidence, assertiveness; courage, boldness, and mettle.

Self-assurance in your own personal judgement, ability, and power. It is future oriented and shows up as the belief that you can figure things out enough to accomplish a goal.

Here's the kicker. You have control over what you believe. You believe in Santa Claus, or you don't. You believe in a Higher Power, or you don't. You believe that the earth is flat, or that it is round. I could go on with examples of the things you may or may not believe. The fact I want to drive home is this: It's your choice.

How do you reclaim your confidence?

You need to tap into your Courage.

Confidence is one thing. Courage is something altogether different. I won't argue the difference between the two concepts. Courage, though, is repeatedly mentioned throughout history as one of the primary virtues of humans. We all possess it to some degree.

COURAGE

What is courage? Rate described it as "...a willful, intentional act, executed under mindful deliberation, involving objective substantial risk to the actor, primarily motivated to bring about a noble good or worthy end, despite, perhaps, the presence of the emotion of fear..." (Rate et al, 2007)

A more poetic, yet powerful, version of courage comes from author and speaker Brene' Brown. "Because true belonging only happens when we present our authentic, imperfect selves to the world, our sense of belonging can never be greater than our level of self-acceptance." She also offers, "**Vulnerability** sounds like truth and feels like **courage**. Truth and **courage** aren't always comfortable, but they're never weakness." [Brown, Daring Greatly...]

How does courage show up in the recovery from a PTS injury?

Let me break it down for you by posing these three questions. First of all, what's the risk to you? Second, what outcome are you looking for? Finally, what do you need to do? The three basic elements of courage, when you have PTSI, can seem so hard to grasp when considered all together.

So, let's walk through the recovery process with these concepts in mind.

RISK

What exactly is the risk to you on your recovery journey? Write it down. Is there more than one thing? Write that down too. Here's a few common ones that I hear both online and in group discussions.

"I don't want to talk about <u>that</u>!! Anything, but <u>that</u>."

"I don't want to take medicine to stabilize my fuckin' mood!!!"

"I can never forgive that asshole for what they did!!! Never!!"

No judgement from me, friend, trust me. I thought them all too. The deeper question is this though:

Where are <u>you</u> holding back?

Here are some of my answers. I didn't want to talk about my suicidal ideation. And I refused to, at first. There were plenty of other things to talk about and work through as I gained trust in my tour guide (aka therapist).

I didn't want to take medicine, and basically refused this as well for over a year. Wait. Let me qualify that: I was willing right from the start to take something for my insomnia because I believed that finally getting several good nights of sleep would do much to alleviate my suffering. Another 18 months would pass before I was willing to try an anti-depressant.

I learned that forgiveness is a process. And it is much less about "that asshole" and what happened in the past, then it is about living in peace today and into the future.

Now that you've weighed the risks of tackling your PTS (mindful deliberation), what's next?

MOTIVATION

Let's look at your motivation. Is it the "noble good" or the "worthy end" that rocks your boat? A combination of both? Motivation often lies outside of us. Are you trying to save your marriage? Spend more quality time with your children? Be a role model to others? What is it? Who is it? Write it down.

I think if your sole motivation is so that you can go back to work, you haven't dug deep enough yet. All careers come to an end, including those within the world of First Responders, either by injury or retirement. All good things must end, right? Don't use your career as your primary motivator to do the work. It's not strong enough to sustain you.

Again, I ask, what is deeply motivating you to tackle the recovery process?

Again, I will share my answers. I am often surprised by how strong I feel about my family. Maybe its generated from the chaos of my youthful days. That was not what I wanted as an adult. I wanted strong, stable relationships. The strongest is the one I have with my husband Curtis.

Sure, we have had our share of ups and downs. All relationships go through that. At the end of the day, we are both grateful to have crossed paths at a Taco Bell in Angel's Camp in the mid 1980's. I knew within a year or so he was someone I wanted in my life for the long-term. I would say 31 years of marriage is long-term, but it almost didn't happen.

Seven years ago, he was having a hard time breathing. What was originally thought to be an asthma flare was actually much worse. He was admitted to the hospital for a series of tests, and after ruling out everything else, including pneumonia, they narrowed it down

to his heart. The plan was to transfer him to the Bay Area the next morning to the health plan's main cardiac facility for additional testing. Knowing he was in good hands, I went home for the evening, and to make plans for animal care. I figured once I got the dogs and cat to the sitters in the morning, I would catch up with him about the time he got out of the scheduled tests.

My sleep was interrupted by an early morning phone call from his doctor. He wasn't stable enough for the transfer to the hospital in San Francisco, so he was sent across town to another hospital with an equally renowned cardiac care program. He was scheduled for an angiogram at 9:00 a.m. I thought it was a win-win situation. He still got the care he needed, and he was closer to home.

By the time I got the critters situated and drove to Santa Rosa, I expected the test to be done with the results soon delivered. What I walked into was anything but routine. He was being prepped for open-heart surgery to replace a valve that was on the brink of failure.

Several hours later I was able to kiss him on the cheek and whisper in his ear, "You are a strong man. Come back to me." A few days later, he did, and I walked into his hospital room one morning to see his handsome smile.

I don't know where I'd be without his strength by my side, but it was my turn to return, to fight my way back.

ACTION

The final discussion point is action-oriented. Make the decision and take action. Pick up the phone and make that appointment. Tell someone you trust. Raise your hand and ask for the help. I don't know what your next right action is.

When you write it down, or add it to your agenda, you are more likely to follow through with it.

What is your next BEST move for your recovery?

Having PTS is not weakness. You've been through a lot. You've seen too much. It shows you are human. Documented symptoms of post-traumatic stress date back to the Battle of Marathon in 490 BC.

Asking for help is perhaps the most courageous action you can take.

<u>CONTROL</u>

As the weeks passed after the fire, I felt stuck. After nearly a month of using sleep medication, I should have felt more rested. I should have felt more satisfaction with my role, my actions on the fire. I should have been able to dredge up some enthusiasm for work. I should have been filled with anticipation for the holidays. This was anything but the truth.

I was in a rut. Higher trained professionals might have called it a deepening depression. I recognized it as a rut. One thing I learned about ruts over the course of my adult life is that once you know it's a rut, quit digging. DO something to climb out of it.

I was moving things around in my home office and picked up a

copy of The Charge (2012), written by Brendon Burchard. I thumbed through it and was reminded again of the human drives that move us. Curious to see what he was up to, I googled him. He was just launching an online course with Oprah Winfrey, "Your Next Bold Move". I was feeling anything but bold at that moment.

What the hell, I thought. Its only 50 bucks. All online. 5 weeks. And it met the requirements I had for breaking out of a rut.

• Break up the routine.

• Learn something new.

We all hit ruts every now and then. It's part of life. Things are just clicking and then they aren't. You can't seem to catch a break. That rut becomes a cave, a cage, a trap. Stay there too long, and it starts sucking at your soul, draining the essence of life.

With PTS, this feeling gets amplified. The average, run-of-the-mill rut becomes something more. The chasm might as well be the Grand Canyon. How do I get back up to the rim? How do I cross over to the other side, where life is happening?

CHARACTER

We already discussed who you believe you are when you are acting from your best self.

Let's take it a step further.

What were your three words again?

Write them down here.

1

2

3

Optimistic mindset

How are you going to take action on your words? What standard are you going to set for yourself?

For instance, this year I am focusing on my creative development. Left to my own devices, not much will happen there. So every week, I go to a watercolor painting class. It gets me out of the house and around other creative people.

Whatever your goal is, it doesn't have to a monumental step. Maybe you want to read more. Maybe it seems overwhelming to read an entire book. I get that. Can you read just one paragraph? Can you make a commitment with yourself to just read one paragraph a day to start with?

You see where I'm going with this? Take your words. What is one small thing you can do every day to take action? Maybe it is just once a week, like my watercolor class? Every little thing you do to get away from what isn't working for you and consciously move towards what might be something better is an action and is commendable.

What are your action steps to breathe life into your words?

NOVELTY

What can you do to break up your routine? Isolation locks us into a routine, or a rut. Your amygdala has your brain convinced that the world is a super scary place. It's another lie called FEAR.

False Evidence Appearing Real

This is where I am going to challenge your isolationist tendencies. You need to go DO something different. Your brain is bored of sitting in your man-cave, looking at the same four walls, day after day after day.

That's not living. That is existing, and you are meant for more than that. Much more than that!

Some ideas to get you started:

- Go to that concert in the park.
- Check out the new restaurant in town.
- Call someone you want to talk to.
- Take your dog for a ride in the country.
- Sign up for music lessons and learn a new technique.
- Plan a weekend getaway for the next month and GO!

What is your plan?

What can you do this week to break out of your rut?

What about within the next 30 days?

Write that down!

Commit to it.

Because the lie of F.E.A.R. can become the truth that you can
Face Everything And Rise!

You deserve to live life to its fullest!

Go LIVE again!

I THINK

Maybe you have heard of this saying,

"I think, therefore I am."

It's true.

What you think about yourself, about your situation, about the people in your life, about your spiritual life, all of that self-talk directs your actions.

If you think you are (BEing) a good person, you will tend to act that way in most situations. You will treat others well, because that is what good people do. If you think poorly of yourself, you tend to act that way too.

The challenge with post-traumatic stress is that the constant influx of stress hormones keeps us on constant alert because the world is deemed to be dangerous. The source of that negative bias lies in a part of the brain you don't have direct control over. In the grand scheme of things, that is actually a solid process. We need to be primed for the fight/flight response in a fraction of a second just in case that shadow in the alley really is a saber-toothed tiger, or the modern version of it. It's necessary for survival.

It's not a good thing though, when you're sitting in your own living room, what you have long considered to be a safe place, and a car backfires outside, or the howling wind announces its presence, and your primitive brain goes straight to 5th gear, causing your anxiety to spin out of control.

With PTS injuries, this is where our brain goes and you may think you can't control that. In reality though, with some training and practice, you can. That is what the recovery process is all about – changing what and how you think about your critical event so you can function in today's world without being in a state of constant high stress.

That howling wind was the first trigger I recognized as such. What's a trigger, you ask? A trigger is something in the environment

(person, place, thing, sound, smell, sight) that causes your brain to say "AHA!!!! LOOK!!! THAT IS DANGEROUS!!! WARNING!!! WARNING!!! WARNING!!!"

It then proceeds to dump an excessive amount of stress hormones into your system, which in turn causes your heart rate, blood pressure, breathing rate, and sweat production to increase drastically. It is not a fun feeling.

How do we counteract the negative? Given our tendency, with PTS, to get saturated with the negative, how do we refocus on the positive, on what is good in our lives?

By being intentional, every day. Planning how we want to show up each day in our life, and the lives of those most important to us. Trust me, it sounds easier than it is. Remember though, that I said recovery is a process. It is a skill set that takes practice on a daily basis.

Break out your journal again. Take a few minutes here to list out ten of your strengths. What makes you one of the good people in the world?

Here's some prompts to get you started:
- What was your best subject in school?
- Can you make children laugh?
- Love animals?
- Have a unique artistic style?
- Play an instrument?
- Take care of your elderly parents?

- Donate time or money to charity?
- Take a complicated subject and break it down so others can understand it?
- Fix your own car?
- Cook a pie from scratch?
- Speak more than one language fluently?

You see, we all have superpowers. You may think it is no big deal to cook a pie from scratch. I can't do it. I love my dogs, but my Spanish is limited to "Mas tequila, por favor." On the other hand, I'm really good at taking a complicated subject and breaking it down so others can understand it. The point is, do not sell yourself short here.

Okay, you have your list done, right?

From that list, pick your top five.

Write them here.

1

2

3

4

5

What would change in your life if you lived from and with your top strengths more often? Not just for one day, but if you practiced your recovery with those strengths consistently in mind for the next week?

The next month?

You see, if you could learn how to do those things well, if you learned how to use those tools, if you learned what a gift you have, before you got injured, then don't you think you have it in you to learn what you need to learn, to practice what you need to practice, for your recovery?

You already know how to get things done. Somebody taught you, or you learned on your own because you were curious enough about that topic. The recovery process is, in essence, learning how to be you again.

INTENTIONS

The exercises I have asked you to do up to this point have been fairly basic, but they are the touchstones of your recovery. I wanted you to reconnect with yourself. I hope that you have.

- The THREE words you are when you are acting from your best version of your SELF.
- Your FIVE strengths.

You needed the reminder. It's that simple.

When left unchecked, Post-Traumatic Stress Injuries push us so far away from our center we no longer recognize ourselves. We end up in uncharted territory, essentially, with no idea how to get back.

Your words and your strengths are part of your navigation system. Consider them your guard rails to stay on the path of your recovery. Now that you have been reminded of them, when you sense yourself drifting off course, or the Incredible Hulk is showing up, tell yourself this...

"That's not who I am."

"I AM" + <u>YOUR</u> THREE WORDS

SCALE UP

Another aspect of PTSI is the overwhelming sense of negativity. I may have mentioned that a time or two. Not because I want to dwell on it. I certainly don't want to do that. Here's the thing, though. We have to acknowledge it so that we understand that we have to be purposeful in our thoughts and actions to counterbalance that negativity. Remember, we can choose what we believe.

Imagine a balance scale with the PTS loaded up on one side with the weight of negativity. Using an intention, what can you do and what can you stop doing to shift the heavy weight of negative and bring more balance to the load?

First of all, whatever you're watching on the television, on YouTube, or Netflix, or whatever other form of social media you engage with, turn it off for a week. Numbing out is a temporary solution to a long-term challenge. Your brain is on hyperdrive. It needs a vacation. Give yourself that gift.

During the week, consider the following question:

What sort of energy does your social media appetite bring in? Is it (A) thoughtful, contemplative, and heartwarming? Or is it (B) divisive, argumentative, and demeaning? Which one, A or B, will do the best job counterbalancing the negativity of your PTS?

You have the responsibility to manage that. I'm not saying you can never, ever, ever again watch media that leans more towards B. What I am asking you to do, while you focus on your recovery, is to practice positivity in all you do. I originally quit drinking alcohol for 90 days because it was going to help with my recovery. Right? What do you need to let go for the next 3-6 months to maximize your recovery efforts?

Remember, I'm a coach. My job, my responsibility, is to challenge people. If you have read this far, you're looking for a path for your recovery. I had to get that negative crap out of my life. I had to be much more purposeful with what I was allowing in.

So, what's your answer? Circle one.

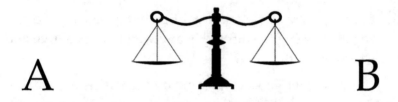

A   B

GRATITUDE

The previous exercise was to get you thinking about how to throttle down the negative inputs to your daily life. Your brain is doing a good enough job at it. It really doesn't need your help.

The next step is more aligned with how you go about filling your life with positive intentions. Actions that will start to add weight to the good side of the scale, the positive side. Removing the negative stops the descent. Our intent here is to increase the value of the positive. One way to do that is to add a Gratitude practice to your daily routine.

I hear you loud and clear. "I have this shitty PTS in my life! And it sucks!!! What the hell do I have to be grateful for?!!"

I used to think the same way. A friend suggested I stop looking inside myself for something to be grateful for. It's a big world, right? When you start looking for the good in it, it changes your perspective. That outside world is where you start your practice.

As you sit on the edge of your bed at night, before your head hits the pillow, I want you to write out three (3) things you are grateful for from your day. What sort of things?

When I first started, I kept it simple. Something I saw in nature. A human interaction. Good music. Art.

On any given day, my gratitude notes could include a squirrel scampering up a tree, witnessing someone holding a door open for a stranger, or watching an artist paint a mural on the side of a building. Another day might include a colorful sunset, the barista smiled at me, or I read something that made me go "Ohhhh, I hadn't thought of it that way before."

This can be a tough assignment, especially if you have reached the professional level of isolation – only leaving your man-cave, home office, or bedroom for a quick bathroom break. If your only interaction with the world happens inside a 10 ft by 10 ft room, you are in jail. The bars of the cell are invisible, but you might as well be on Alcatraz in solitary confinement. To break the pattern, to find things to be grateful for, you have to get outside of yourself, and engage with the three-dimensional world.

For a while, I really struggled with this. I didn't even want to leave my house to go have Sunday brunch with my friends, something I had been doing consistently for the last eight years. Sometimes it takes anger to get moving, and if that is what it takes for you to step outside of the house, then get angry. I know I had to.

The chief in me had to take control of the situation. "This is stupid Linda! Go for a walk around the block!! It's not like you have never done this before!!! Get your ass out of the house!!!!!" Nobody likes being yelled at, including me, but that's where I had to go to move.

The funny thing is, after about a week of forcing myself to go for that walk, I began to look forward to it. I started to enjoy the daily quest for the beauty of the world. Sometimes I would walk to the local coffee shop, order my favorite beverage, and people watch. Other times I walked downtown and explored, or I would sit in the park and watch the kids play.

I came to realize that life goes on, and I wanted more of it than what being an isolationist was providing me. In fact, I began to feel moments of real peace noticing all the beauty around me.

Enough about me though. Let's get back to you. As you go about your day, pay more attention to what is happening around you.

Even if the extent of your foray into the real world is standing on the porch with one hand on the door, ready for a rapid retreat back inside. What did you notice? And how did that make you feel?

What three things are you grateful for today?

1 _____

2 _____

3 _____

Awesome!

Now, go out there and practice being a good human.

I AM CONNECTED

Humans are social creatures. Whether you're an introvert or extrovert, a reggae musician or a nuclear scientist, or an interior decorator or emergency responder, we all need other people in our lives. The strength of those connections keeps our hearts open to possibility. We have the opportunity to laugh and to love. We can share our collective knowledge and take a real picture of a black hole or find a cure for cancer. Connections matter, the moment we are born un-

til the day we die. Things are nice. Connections, though, are pure energy.

Post-traumatic stress injuries corrode our connections. As our own energy is diverted to just surviving day to day, the connections to our friends weaken. Your family no longer knows who to expect home for dinner - Dr. Jekyll or Mr. Hyde? Your co-workers are perplexed by your behavior, and give you space, thinking that maybe you're having a bad day.

The problem is, that bad day turns into a bad week, and then into a bad month. You may not even be aware of it. The shift is subtle at first. After a while, though, it's hard to ignore the change.

A few months after the fire. I got home from work, only to find my usual parking spot partially blocked by my sister's car. By the time I walked in the front door, I was seething, and exploded on the first person I saw. The parking situation was a minor inconvenience. My anger was raw, and fearsome, even to me.

After I changed clothes, I left the house. Partially because I was still angry, and perhaps, even more so, embarrassed by my own behavior. Like, where the hell did that come from? My walk took me to my favorite neighborhood pub. I ordered the chocolate stout, and pondered life while I cooled off. I eventually called my brother for a lift home, not realizing he was halfway across the county at the time.

When he arrived, I bought him a pint, and had myself a second stout for good order. I explained what had happened, as best I could. In his own loving way, he called me an idiot. I had to admit he was right. I had crossed the line of acceptable behavior within our family dynamic. I believe firmly in the Golden Rule, and I had just committed a felony level violation of its principle.

I took responsibility for my poor behavior and apologized to my family the next day. But the anger continued. I would come home from work, and just be pissed off. I went straight to my bedroom on more than one occasion and tossed the room. I felt like the Incredible Hulk. I don't know who was scared more, me or my family.

A couple weeks later I discussed this scenario with my therapist. Here's the bottom line. Don't take it out on your family. Or your friends. Or your dog. They're not the enemy.

GROUNDED

What I would like you to do now is to think about the relationships you have. Your family. Friends. Co-workers.

You already went through the exercise to describe yourself – how you act when you are coming from the aspect of your BEST self. If you haven't done so yet, pause here and go back to that exercise.

Thank you for doing that. I think it's important that you acknowledge your role in fostering relationships, and that includes the one you have with yourself.

Okay, now what I want you to do is to think about your relationships. How do you want to interact with each of them? I'll give you a couple of examples. With people I don't know that well, at the very least I want to be in alignment with the Golden Rule, so I remind myself to treat everyone with compassion and understanding. I don't know if someone is always a jerk or is just having a bad day. It's my choice though, to be kind. And maybe even smile at that them.

With my husband, I want to be patient, and fun-loving. I want to have meaningful conversations with him. I want to explore the world, with him by my side. My PTS almost destroyed my 30-year relationship with this man whom I love. I'm taking a much more purposeful route now, no longer taking it for granted.

You can also apply this principle to other parts of your life. What role do you want to take in your community? What sort of environment do you want to create for your family to live in? What is your personal manifesto?

Some of this may seem overwhelming or even confusing. I get it. Things may be pretty ugly in your life right now in. You think you may have damaged some relationships beyond repair. That may be so. Or, you may be wearing blinders, and can't see, let alone <u>feel</u>, the love you are wrapped in.

Either way you have to start a project, and recovery from PTS is a project, with the end in mind. I'm not always a happy-go-lucky person. I still have bad days, filled with anxiety and/or depression. The difference now, compared to a couple years ago, is my approach to each and every conversation I have with the people that are important to me. Every day, I think about how I want to show up. With my young grand-nephews, I get to be the race car driver, the goofy aunt, or the brilliant conversationalist. With my sister, I can be the brat of the family, or the rock of Gibraltar. As a peer, I hold space for others. As an author, I inspire.

I don't always hit a home run. Sometimes I strike out. Sometimes I have to adjust my approach. That's life though and I think with or without PTS we all need to adjust ourselves at time throughout life.

When you allow yourself to be tossed about by the storms of life, regardless of the source of the storm, you're not living. You're surviving. When you take back hold of the steering wheel, and start moving with intention, you start regaining control.

How do you want to interact with your spouse or significant other?

What three words describe that?

Why?

How do you want to interact with your children?

What three words describe that?

Why?

How do you want to interact with your brothers/sisters?

What three words describe that?

Why?

Parents? Aunts and Uncles?

What three words describe that?

Why?

Your best friends?

What three words describe that?

Why?

Your buddies at work?

What three words describe that?

Why?

If you have never thought about it before, now is as good a time as any.

Start with the end in mind.

Do This:

You need to remind yourself every day of how you want to treat people. I wrote my three words for the relationship with my husband on a 3x5 card and stuck it in the visor of my truck. Once I parked the truck in the driveway, I would pull out that card and read my words out loud. When my hand touched the doorknob of the front door of the house, I silently reminded myself of my intentions, and smiled as I walked in.

Words are powerful.

Use them well and reap the rewards.

The Common Thread

From top to bottom, through every vein, through every breath we take runs one common element. I almost don't feel qualified to talk about it. As with many people, I have been debating the issue for a few decades.

Do I have a soul?

I was not brought up with a religious background. Although both of my parents had been raised within the Christian faith, they couldn't agree on which facet to raise their children in. Other than my sister, we did not attend church.

I was in the fifth grade before I ever heard of the Golden Rule:

"Do unto others as you would have them do unto you."

As I thought about it for the next day or two, I realized it was actually a good way to live, and I adopted it as my first ever standard to live my life by.

In high school, I witnessed the hypocrisy of my fellow students, and developed a somewhat jaded viewpoint of organized religion. In junior college, I fell in with a crowd of believers, and listened and felt the strength of their beliefs, eventually accepting Jesus as my savior. My follow-up was non-existent though. Although I was married in a church, I never did the work to deepen my understanding of what it meant to be spiritual.

After my injury, I honestly felt that perhaps my injury happened because of the lack of belief in a higher power, my lack of a spiritual practice.

I have since changed my mind. Lillie Leonardi wrote about her journey with PTSD following the events of 9/11. (In the Shadow of a Badge) As an FBI agent she responded to the Pennsylvania crash site in Shanksville. Despite her strong life-long religious beliefs and practices, she still developed PTS. If someone as devout as her could be injured, then perhaps religion had nothing to do with it.

The question of my soul was finally answered in one of the first sessions I had for EMDR. I explained to Lori that I understood

the facts of the situation in my brain, at an intellectual level, but I couldn't feel it in my soul, in my heart. There was a disconnect. And I had no idea how to integrate the two.

I believe that we are each on a unique spiritual path. I don't believe in any particular dogma. I'm at a place in my life now where I have the time and energy to be curious enough to explore what that means to me. I used to be agnostic. I openly admit that.

My injury though, has forced me to reevaluate that position. I now believe that the Universe has something to offer, if I'm open to receiving it. So, I'm remaining curious and openminded. I'm exploring. It's my journey, and I don't expect anyone else to follow my exact footprints.

I'm just asking you to return to that time in your life when you felt awe and wonder as the world unfolded before you and pick up the trail of exploration again.

I covered a lot of ground in this section. I talked about courage, congruency, and connections. I shared my life model of the tree with you. I challenged you to be curious. I challenged you to take action. I challenged you to get the hell out of your man-cave! I challenged you to care again about the connections in your life.

We are social creatures. We belong in the world.

YOU belong in the world.

Go claim your place!

Call To Action

Why?

I get asked WHY an awful lot.

"Why are you hurting yourself, day after day?"

"Why are you doing all of this crazy stuff?"

"But you're retired! Haven't you done enough?"

"Hasn't your Post-Traumatic Stress Injury cost you too much already?"

My answer?

Because...

I hurt even more when I hear about another suicide.

All of this "crazy stuff" keeps me sane.

How do you define "enough"?

My "injury" has made me stronger.

Wiser.

More complete.

The fact is, every time I share my story, and one person takes the time to engage, and listen, and think, that is more time for them on the face of this earth.

That is more time for them to nurture hope.

That is more time for them to engage with their recovery process.

That is more time for them to LIVE.

That is more time for them to make a difference in another person's life.

My "ripple effect" will save lives.

It may have already.

Honestly, some people think I shouldn't be doing this stuff.

I almost believed them.

I almost stayed in that small place that says, "In Service to Others".

I was recently asked what went through my mind at 3 o'clock in the morning, when the tones went off at the fire station?

It's a call to duty, was my reply.

CALL TO DUTY

I don't know about you.

But I can't ignore that call.

That's why I share my story.

That's why I talk about HOPE.

That's why I talk about COURAGE.

That's why I talk about GRATITUDE.

That's why I talk about COMMITMENT.

That's why I do what I do.

Too many cops. Too many firefighters. Too many paramedics.

Too many correctional officers. Too many emergency dispatchers

Too many veterans.

Too many families.

Too many suicides.

Too many destroyed lives that affects <u>generations</u>.

It's my CALL TO DUTY.

Are you with me?

~ Linda Green ~

February 12, 2019

Afterword

BRAIN INJURY – THE DEBATE

I'm looking forward to the results of current testing that is specifically trying to determine exactly where PTSI impacts neural pathways. When science can show exactly where that disruption to the neural pathway is or, in fact that pre-existing neural pathways have been destroyed because of the effect of stress, that will add some weight to the injury argument.

Given that psychiatric diagnoses are based mostly on subjective symptom clusters, the development of objective testing measures will help on many fronts. Not only will it help the injured person directly demonstrating that in fact, there is something amiss, but also do much to reduce the stigma that is associated with PTSI.

Think about it. When a body part is hurt, that makes it an injury and redefining PTS as an injury instead of a disorder will lead the way in reducing the stigma.

When somebody can put all this together, and say, "Here are the facts, and get off your high horse of your stigma", it will change the discussion. Look what happened with cancer. Back in the 1960s and 70s cancer was that big, scary thing. That "C" word was not discussed openly. As research led to better treatment protocols, and survivability, people opened up about their struggles with cancer. Now cancer is part of everyday conversations. Don't get me wrong. That diagnosis is still scary, because no one treatment works for all cancers.

The difference is that cancer has become part of the common language. People report anomalies to their doctor sooner, which leads to better outcomes. I believe all of this research that's going on will help in the same way with post-traumatic stress.

A picture paints a thousand words, right? Being able to *show* people that there is really something going on will change perceptions. It is not just somebody malingering trying to get out of work or trying to game the system. You can't game the system with a blood test that shows the biomarkers of psychological stress. You can't game the system when you go in for an EEG sleep study. You most certainly can't game the system over 20 years and have your brain structure significantly change. You can't game the system with machine learning.

The real game changer, though, is the development of objective testing protocols. They can't go mainstream fast enough.

FUTURE OF DIAGNOSTIC TESTING

One of the challenges with post-traumatic stress is that it has been based on subjective reporting by the people who are so afflicted with it. As such, it is hard for some people to believe that post-traumatic stress is actually causing as much distress as someone says it is. This leads to delays in seeking treatment, stigma, or not following treatment protocols.

There are several recent reports about PTS that I believe will help drive it from being a purely subjective self-report of the symptoms, to something that can actually be objectively measured and confirmed by the medical community.

Because this injury is invisible, supervisors may think that people are faking it, or malingering. People who are suffering from post-traumatic stress - because it's such a subjective thing - may actually not fully engage with their own treatment process, because they can't see test results that confirm the diagnosis. It's like, this is how I *feel*. And somebody says, well, based on how you think you're feeling, this is what I think you have, and it leaves the diagnosis in that nebulous area. It's a lot of gray matter.

Recent research findings may help clarify that fuzzy area between objective and subjective, helping to move PTSI out of the world of stigma. All of the following studies were reported on in the first quarter of 2019: identifiable biomarkers of psychological stress, measurable sleep disruptions via EEG, long-term changes to brain structures using sMRI, and differentiating between healthy and stressed individuals using machine learning. This diversity of testing options that, once developed for wide use, will help confirm the diagnosis to the injured person, develop more targeted treatments, and destigmatize PTSD.

The first report talked about objective predictive gene expression biomarkers. What they're looking for with these biomarkers are signs of psychological stress due to environmental adversity versus that caused by stress created by having a heart attack or being diagnosed with cancer. Researchers were looking for metabolic and hormonal changes to identify the biological roots of the subjective symptoms by looking at specific areas of gene expression.

In the process, they identified the best biomarkers for involvement in stress. Their goal was to better identify and not only confirm the diagnosis of that psychological stress, but also the most appropriate drug to provide for treatment. It is encouraging to know that in the future someone can take a blood test and not only know that they are in fact injured, but they can also be prescribed the most appropriate medication based on which biomarker is showing up. (Le-Niculescu et al, 2019)

The second report discussed a sleep study utilizing EEG (electroencephalography). Most people with post-traumatic stress have sleep disorders. The intent of the study was to determine if there was a difference in sleep between healthy, non-trauma exposed people and PTS injured people. What they found was a strong correlation between people in their awake state, when they're in non REM2 stage into sleep. When they tested people with PTS against non-trauma exposed healthy individuals, they were also able to show a very strong correlation with sleep disturbances on the EEG results. (Modarres et al, 2019)

The third study compared brain imaging of a group of veterans over the span of 24 years. The first scan was done after they had been diagnosed with PTSI. At a follow-up 24 years later, with that same cohort, they did another brain scan using structural magnetic resonance imaging (sMRI).

They compared the two looking for any volume changes in brain structure within different components of the brain. Researchers did in fact, find lower hippocampal, amygdala, rostral middle frontal gyrus, and medial orbitofrontal cortex volumes. Their findings are sobering. "Even at sub-diagnostic threshold levels, PTS symptoms were present decades after trauma exposure in parallel with highly correlated structural deficits in brain regions regulating stress responsivity and adaptation." (Franz et al, 2019)

Finally, using a support vector machine learning system, researchers wanted to determine if they could differentiate symptoms between healthy and injured individuals. They tested three study groups: those diagnosed with post-traumatic stress, trauma-exposed people that had not been diagnosed with post-traumatic stress, and a healthy control group. What they showed with the machine learning is that they could differentiate with up to 80% accuracy between people with post-traumatic stress and the healthy control group based on a sleep study. The accuracy was about 70% between the post-traumatic stress group and the trauma-exposed group on not only sleep measurements, but also with memory testing. With some refinement, this is going to improve the diagnostic accuracy and treatment protocols for people with PTSI. (Breen et al, 2019)

AS FOR ME...

As I finish writing this book, some things have become very obvious, even to me. I understand this recovery work is never a "cure", never completely done and always an effort.

This past Monday we put Macy down. We had rescued her from a ranch about 10 years ago and given her to my mom. After Mom died in the fall of 2014, we brought Macy back with us. She was old then, and we didn't think she would make it to see another year. Macy had more heart than we gave her credit for. Surrounded by a younger pack of dogs (and people) Macy bounced back. She was happy and loved. We knew in August 2018 that she was not going to see another summer and made her as comfortable as possible. The morning we took her to the vet for the last time, I took a picture of her. As I looked at the picture later in the day, I could see the fatigue in her eyes. She was done.

I didn't cry for her, just felt sorrow. I certainly didn't get any work done that day. Later in the week, when Davis PD Officer Natalie Corona was gunned down, I didn't cry for her either. And on Thursday, when I could feel my brain wrapped in the grip of mental fog, I knew something had to give.

In mid-December I started an experiment with my supplement regime. I quit taking them. I had improved my diet enough to lose 40 pounds, and I wanted to see if the diet improvement was enough to offset my brain injury. Within a week I recognized the daily presence of anxiety and the inability to focus. I went back on the gaba/tyrosine dosage in the morning.

Between Christmas and the New Year, my diet was holding relatively steady, and I was able to maintain my weight. As I cycled back into my routine for losing fat, I really noticed the difference that the lack of supplementation was having on me. Motivation was nil. Intentionality was missing in action. My sleep routine slid backwards into the wee hours of the morning. The spark I had in early December had been doused.

Physical health starts with brain health. I recognize that I am in a depressive cycle right now. I also recognize that the supplements were giving me a new lease on life. Yesterday I refilled my packs. Hopefully I will notice the improvement in another day or two. Like Macy, I'm not ready to throw in the towel.

I could be totally self-loathing right now, thinking it was pretty stupid to quit something that was working. But I'm not. Eventually I would try to go without the supplements. I needed to know where I stood. Obviously, I'm not ready yet. I may never be able to enjoy life without those daily reminders that all is not well with my brain. It is what it is.

Grant me the SERENITY to accept the things I cannot change

COURAGE to change the things I can

And the WISDOM to know the difference.

-Reinhold Neibuhr

When I started on this recovery journey from my post-traumatic stress injury, I swore to myself that I would try anything to beat it. I didn't care if it was experimental or not. I haven't had to go that far, yet.

I'm not taking anything off the list of possibilities. It's not that I'm being selfish here. The fact is, I am more than worthy enough to fight for my next breath.

Here's why.

Every day I have the possibility of helping someone improve their life whether it be an issue with alcoholism, or post-traumatic stress. Every day I have the opportunity to be of service. Every day, as I think of my family and friends, I am reminded of the far-reaching effects of the ripples generated by my presence, by my being present.

My hope for you is that you become an agent of change, whether it is on a personal or professional level. We all have the ability to level up in our lives. We all have the strength to do the hard work. We all are worthy of taking the next best step forward.

Courage is not the absence of fear.

Courage is trust.

Courage is faith.

Courage is innate in all of us.

When the mission is big enough, courage shows up, flexes its muscles, puts a steadying hand on your shoulder, and says...

"Let's Go!"

RESOURCES
REFERENCES
&
READER REFLECTIONS

Resources

This is not a comprehensive list. Consider it a starting point. I will continue to add new and updated information in future editions of this book.

12-step Programs for Recovery

Alcoholics Anonymous: www.aa.org/

Narcotics Anonymous: www.na.org/

Overeaters Anonymous: oa.org/groupsservice-bodies/world-service/

Gamblers Anonymous: www.gamblersanonymous.org/ga/content/about-us

Books Written by People Who Have PTSD, and Lived to Tell Their Story

Buckley, Jacqueline, CD BA. Eye of The Storm: Personal Commitment To Managing Symptoms Of PTSD. iUniverse LLC. Bloomington IN USA. 2014

[Dental technician – SwissAir Flight 111 crash, 1998]

Campbell, Jamie. The Forgetten Few. Self-published 2016

[Correctional officer]

Harris, Natalie. Save-My-Life School: A First Responder's Mental Health Journey. Wintertinkle Press, Barrie ON. 2017

[Paramedic – Ontario Canada]

Haskin, Leslie. Between Heaven And Ground Zero. Bethany House. Minneapolis, MN. 2006

[Civilian – Insurance industry – World Trade Center, 9/11]

Horwitz, Samantha. The Silent Fall: A Secret Service Agent's Story of Tragedy and Triumph after 9/11. Courage to Win LLC. 2016

[Law Enforcement – Secret Service – World Trade Center, 9/11]

Leonardi, Lillie. In The Shadow Of A Badge: A Memoir About Flight 93, A Field Of Angels, And My Spiritual Homecoming. Hay House. 2013

[Law Enforcement – FBI – Shanksville, Pennsylvania crash site, 9/11]

PTSD Retreats – United States

Deer Hollow: www.ptsdandtraumadrugrehab.com/

First Responders Support Network (FRSN). www.frsn.org

International Association of Firefighters (IAFF). Center for Excellence: www.iaffrecoverycenter.com/

Warriors Heart: First Responders and Military: www.warriorsheart.com/

PTSD Retreats – Canada

Terence Joseph Kosikar: campmyway.com/

Facebook communities

Note: This is only a sampling of what is available within the world of Facebook. I share all this just so you know – you're not alone.

911 Help Site:
www.facebook.com/groups/911HelpSite/

A Spouse's Story PTSD
www.facebook.com/ASpousesStoryPTSD/

Butters – My PTSD Fire Dog
www.facebook.com/ButtersthePTSDfiredog/

Project Hope: EMS, PTSD:
www.facebook.com/rescuingourown/

PTSD Break the Silence
www.facebook.com/ptsdbreakthesilence/

PTSD Bunker Gear for Your Brain:
www.facebook.com/PTSDBunkerGearForYourBrain/

PTSD in Paramedics, EMTs, First Responders:
www.facebook.com/firstaid4heroes/

PTSD Journal

www.facebook.com/PTSDJournal/

PTSD Projects

www.facebook.com/PTSDProjects/

Surviving the Shield: PTSD and Public Safety

www.facebook.com/survivingtheshield/

Uniformed Services Peer Council

www.facebook.com/USPCCT/

Podcasts

Uptalk Podcast with Sean Conohan

"Season 4 – Episode 3" (2019):

itunes.apple.com/us/podcast/uptalk-podcast-s4e3-dr-megan-mcelheran/id1076465971?i=1000431357465&mt=2

PTSD Bunker Gear for Your brain – with Carl Wagget

Running nonstop since

"A PTSD TIP…We all need somebody ;)" (March 21, 2019)

itunes.apple.com/us/podcast/a-ptsd-tip-we-all-need-somebody/id1206636820?i=1000432695753&mt=2

Rescue the Rescuer

Hosted by Steve Kavalovich

"Food and Mental Health with Danny Mills" (March 6, 2019)

itunes.apple.com/us/podcast/food-and-mental-health-with-danny-mills/id1267632031?i=1000433012160&mt=2

Suicide Organizations and Hotlines

In the USA: Call: 1-800-273-8255

Text: 741741

TTY: 1-800-799-4889

Espanol: 1-888-628-9454

Veterans Crisis Line: Text 838255

International Association for Suicide Prevention

www.iasp.info/resources/Crisis_Centres/

National Suicide Prevention Lifeline

suicidepreventionlifeline.org/

Suicide.org

Provides a state by state listing of hotlines

www.suicide.org/suicide-hotlines.html

Suicide Stop: International Help Center

International crisis numbers

www.suicidestop.com/call_a_hotline.html

Organizations

FFBHA

www.ffbha.org/

Code 9 Project

www.code9project.org/

Blue HELP

bluehelp.org/

REFERENCES

Section 1

My personal notes

Section 2

Author unknown. Firefighter's Prayer.
www.aspiringfirefighters.com/coaching/firemans-prayer/

Green, Linda. Webinar: The Valley Fire 2015. Hosted online by California Fire Science Consortium. www.youtube.com/watch?v=E-_C79Fk7Xg 2016

Section 3

Alcoholics Anonymous World Services, Inc. *Alcoholics Anonymous: The story of how many thousands of men and women have recovered from alcoholism*, Fourth Edition. New York. Print. 2001

Alcoholics Anonymous World Services, Inc. *Daily reflections: A book of reflections by A.A. members for A.A. members*. New York. 1990

AA Grapevine, Inc. *Emotional Sobriety II: The Next Frontier*. AA Grapevine, Inc. New York. Print. 2011

ABC 7 News. Investigators: massive Valley Fire caused by faulty hot tub wiring. abc7news.com/news/massive-valley-fire-caused-by-faulty-hot-tub-wiring/1464779/ Web. August 10, 2016.

Amen Clinics, Inc. Brain health assessment: What's your brain type? brainhealthassessment.com/

Amen, Daniel C., MD. *Healing ADD: The breakthrough program that allows you to see and heal the 7 types of ADD*. Penguin, New York. Print. 2013

Amen, Daniel C. MD. *Change your brain: Change your life*. Penguin, New York. Print. 2015

American Psychiatric Association. *Diagnostic and Statistical Manual of Mental Disorders*, Fifth Edition. Arlington, VA, American Psychiatric Association. Print. 2013

Beachbody. Tai cheng. www.beachbody.com/product/fitness_ programs/tai-cheng-workout.do

Beachbody. T-25 workout. www.beachbody.com/product/fitness_programs/focus-t25-workout-mobile.do

Burchard, Brendon. Bring the joy. www.youtube.com/ watch?v=sMbeQMlRxbs. Video. 2016

Burchard, Brendon. *The motivation manifesto: 9 declarations to claim your personal power.* New York. Hay House. Print. 2014

California Department of Forestry & Fire Protection. Investigation report – redacted. www.calfire.ca.gov/fire_protection/downloads/FireReports/Valley/15CALNU0008670_Valley_Redacted. pdf Web. August, 2016.

Cardinal, Sherry LCSW. What is CISM? CISM International website. www.criticalincidentstress.com/what_is_cism_

Conohan, Sean. Uptalk Podcast with Sean Conohan. Season 4 – Episode 3. itunes.apple.com/us/podcast/uptalk-podcast-s4e3-dr-megan-mcelheran/id1076465971?i=1000431357465& mt=2. 2016

Lake County Peg TV. Know Lake County – Valley Fire Panel. youtu.be/bm_FsBASesY. May 8, 2016

Lansing, Karen M. LMFT. *The rite of return: Coming back from duty-induced PTSD.* High Ground Press. Kindle. 2012

Mackey, Jill. Where women create. Volume 9, Issue 1. Pg. 93. Print. 2017

Schultz, Charles M. *Happiness is a warm puppy*. Determined Productions. San Francisco. Print. 1962

Section 4

Breen, M.S., Thomas, K.G.F., Baldwin, D.S., & Lipinska, G. Modelling PTSD diagnosis using sleep, memory, and adrenergic metabolites: An exploratory machine-learning study. Human Psychopharmacology: Clinical & Experimental (vol32/iss2). Wiley Online Library. February 22, 2019. doi.org/10.1002/hup.2691

Franz, C.E., Hatton, S.N., Hauger, R.L. et al. Abstract: Posttraumatic stress symptom persistence across 24 years: association with brain structures. Brain Imaging and Behavior (2019). Springer US. doi.org/10.1007/s11682-019-00059-x

Le-Niculescu, H., Rosberry, K., Levey, d.F., et al. Towards precision medicine for stress disorders: diagnostic biomarkers and targeted drugs. Molecular psychiatry. Springer Nature Publishing AG. March 12, 2019. doi.org/10.1038/s41380-019-0370-z

Mad TV. New Therapy with Bob Newhart and Mo Collins. Episode 6.24. Originally aired May 12, 2001. www.youtube.com/watch?v=PHTzYDbkkfU

Modarres, MH. Opel, RA. Weymann KB. Lim MM. Strong correlation of novel sleep electroencephalography coherence markers with diagnosis and severity of posttraumatic stress disorder. Scientific Reports – Nature Publishing Group. London, 2019 March 12; 9(1):4247 doi.org/10.1038/s41598-018-38102-4

Moore, H.M., Rogers, E., Greenlee, W., & Marino, S. New Florida law expands PTSD benefits for first responders, but is it enough? Treasure Coast Newspapers. Florida, USA, Online. March 22, 2019 www.tcpalm.com/story/news/local/2019/03/22/ptsd-law-first-responders-suicide/2511959002/

Section 6

Brown, Brene'. *Daring greatly: How the courage to be vulnerable transforms the way we live, love, parent, and lead.* Avery. Print. 2015

Burchard, Brendon. *The charge: activating the 10 human drives that make you feel alive.* New York. Free Press, 2012

Leonardi, Lillie. *In the shadow of a badge: A memoir about Flight 93, a field of angels, and my spiritual homecoming.* Hay House. Print. 2013

Rate, C.R., Clarke, J.A., Lindsay, D.R. & Sternberg , R.J. (2007) Implicit theories of courage, The Journal of Positive Psychology, 2:2, 80-98, DOI: 10.1080/17439760701228755

ALL

Avsec, Robert & Michaud, Nathalie, & Brooks, Will, & Green, Linda. *Essays on Firefighters and Post Traumatic Stress: Selected posts from Talking Shop 4 Fire and EMS,* Kindle Edition www.amazon.com/dp/B07217X27W

Brown, Brene'. *Daring greatly: How the courage to be vulnerable transforms the way we live, love, parent, and lead.* Avery. Print. 2015

Buckley, Jacqueline, CD BA. *Eye Of The Storm: Personal Commitment To Managing Symptoms Of PTSD.* iUniverse LLC. Bloomington IN USA. 2014

Burchard, Brendon. *The motivation manifesto: 9 declarations to claim your personal power.* New York. Hay House. Print. 2014

Chapman, Gary. *The 5 love Languages: The secret to love that lasts.* Northfield Publishing. 2015

Colman, David. Challenging the second A in AA. The New York Times. Fashion & Style section. May 2011 www.nytimes.com/2011/05/08/fashion/08anon.html

Conflagration – Definition. en.wikipedia.org/wiki/Conflagration

Coyhis, Don L. *Meditations with Native American Elders: The Four Seasons.* Colorado Springs, CO, USA. Coyhis Publishing & Consulting, Inc. 2007

Dissociation and Dissociative Disorders. Mental Health America website. 2019 www.mentalhealthamerica.net/conditions/dissociation-and-dissociative-disorders

Edmund, Bryan. The Sobriety Network: A Recovery Podcast with Bryan Edmund. Episode 31. www.stitcher.com/podcast/the-sobriety-network-with-bryan-edmund. Podcast. July 24, 2016

EMDR International Association www.emdria.org/page/emdr_therapy

Faces and Voices of Recovery, org. Stigma reduction. facesandvoicesofrecovery.org/what-we-do/stigma-reduction/

Fay, J., Kamena, M. D., Benner, A., Buscho, A. & Nagle, D. Emergency responder exhaustion syndrome (ERES): A perspective on stress, coping and treatment in the emergency responder milieu. www.frsn.org/Resources/articles

FIRESCOPE. About Us. 2019 firescope.caloes.ca.gov/about-us.htm

Frankl, Viktor E. *Man's Search for Meaning*. Beacon Press, Boston. Print. 1959.. 2006

Goldberg, Natalie and Cameron, Julie. *Writing Down the Bones: Freeing the Writer Within*. Shambala Publications, Boulder CO, 1986

Gwinn, Casey, JD & Hellman, Chan Ph.D. *Hope rising: How the science of hope can change your life.* New York. Morgan James. 2019

Harris, Natalie. *Save-My-Life School: A first responder's mental health journey.* Wintertinkle Press, Barrie ON. 2017

Haskin, Leslie. *Between heaven and ground zero.* Bethany House. Minneapolis, MN. 2006

Horwitz, Samantha. *The silent fall: A secret service agent's story of tragedy and triumph after 9/11.* Courage to Win LLC. 2016

Kirschman, E.; Fay, J.; Kamena, M. *Counseling cops: What clinicians need to know.* The Guilford Press. New York. 2014

Lipton, Bruce H. Ph.D. *The biology of belief: Unleashing the power of consciousness, matter, and miracles.* – 10th anniversary edition. New York. Hay House. Print. 2005

Mad TV. New Therapy with Bob Newhart and Mo Collins. Episode 6.24. Originally aired May 12, 2001. www.youtube.com/watch?v=PHTzYDbkkfU

Mammatus clouds. Names of Clouds website. 2019 www.namesofclouds.com/types-of-clouds/mammatus-clouds.html

Moore, H.M., Rogers, E., Greenlee, W., & Marino, S. New Florida law expands PTSD benefits for first responders, but is it enough? Treasure Coast Newspapers, Florida, USA. Online. March 22, 2019 www.tcpalm.com/story/news/local/2019/03/22/ptsd-law-first-responders-suicide/2511959002/

National Institute of Standards and Technology. Ember Exposure Characterization in WUI Fires Project. NIST.gov February 28, 2016   www.nist.gov/programs-projects/ember-exposure-characterization-wui-fires-project

National Wildfire Coordinating Group (NWCG) Leading in the Wildland Fire Service. PMS 494-2 (NFES #002889) January 2007 www.nwcg.gov/publications/494-2

National Wildfire Coordinating Group (NWCG). Glossary – foehn wind. www.nwcg.gov/term/glossary/foehn-wind%C2%A0'

Needleman, Jacob & Piazza, John P. *The Essential Marcus Aurelius*: translated and introduced by Jacob Needleman and John P. Piazza. Tarcher Cornerstone Editions. New York. Penguin. Print. 2008

Ortiz, Deborah Louise. Documentary: *Code 9: Officer Needs Assistance*. Code 9 Project. 2015. Official trailer available at www.youtube.com/watch?v=VkqFjvoa6iQ

Parekh, Ranna, MD, MPH. What is Posttraumatic Stress Disorder? American Psychiatric Association website. January 2017 www.psychiatry.org/patients-families/ptsd/what-is-ptsd

Positive Psychology Program website: 5 Worksheets for challenging negative automatic thoughts (+PDF). March 16, 2018. www.positivepsychologyprogram.com/challenging-automatic-thoughts-positive-thoughts-worksheets/

Van der Kolk, Bessel A. *The body keeps the score: brain, mind, and body in the healing of trauma*. New York. Penguin Books. Print. 2014

Transcription services provided by Otter Voice Notes AISense.com, Los Altos, CA 2019 www.aisense.com/

READER REFLECTIONS

ACKNOWLEDGMENTS

This story doesn't get told without the support of too many people to count, let alone name in this section. However, there are some I would like to call attention to.

My many talented Facilitative Tour Guides through that mass of gray cells and neural connections called my Brain: Dr. Anne Kopp, Ph.D.; Dr. Judith Phillips Sill, Ph.D.; and Laura Capinis, LCSW. Thank you for unlocking the cage and letting me be free again.

To the First Responder Support Network: All of the peers, clinicians, and chaplains. Ellen "Columbo" Kirschman, Ph.D. and Nan Herron, MD., the two clinicians at my retreat. At the time, I really hated that "Be curious" mantra. It grew on me though. Nick Turkovich - for allowing your compassion to shine on that first phone call. Mahalo! The Honey Badgers - you know who you are! I love you all!

CAL FIRE, in particular, the Employee Support Services (ESS) personnel. Michael Ming, Davina Sentak, Steve Diaz, Shawna Powell, Tony Howard and all the rest. You are tremendously underfunded and understaffed for such an important mission. It's bad enough that cancer takes too many too soon. Stress kills too. I hope this book helps.

Tim brah'… for replying to that midnight text, meeting me for coffee, sharing your story, and pointing me in the right direction.

Equally important, my brothers and sisters from other mothers and misters. Although the CAL FIRE family numbers in the thousands, I want to give a special shout out to the Crabtree and the Vallerga families. You welcomed me into your worlds years ago, and allowed me to stay even when I was not truly "present".

The First Responders (Fire, LEO, EMS, CDCR) throughout the greater Sonoma-Lake-Napa Unit of CAL FIRE. It was my honor and privilege to work alongside some of the most dedicated people on the face of this planet.

The Certified High Performance Coaching and Growth communities. Who knew that watching a geeky young man share his productivity planning page on a YouTube video in the early 2000's would lead me here? Thank you, Brendon Burchard, for being a bright star to the world. Your light drew me in, fed me, nurtured me, and lifted me up. Special shout-out to Michelle Hujiev. How blessed was I to have you as my first coach?

My coaching friends and supporters. Thank you for guiding me back and pushing me forward. For lifting me up and encouraging me to soar. For your patience when my brain wouldn't fire and helping me to fill my cup. For reminding me that I am, indeed, smart enough to figure things out. And that it's okay to "feel" as part of the human condition.

The Amen Clinics and Dr. Daniel Emina MD for those informative SPECT scans of my brain, and the strategy to get it back on track, and Belldon Colme for teaching me about the Zen of food.

The greater Internet community, Facebook groups related to PTSD, and the Jungle. Many of you work in relative obscurity, driven only by your passion to help. I have never met most of you in person, let alone spoken with you on the phone. But without your support in those dark days, this story would not continue;

Everything book related:

Carolyn Flower and the Oxygen Publishing House. Chappie Steve for the brilliant cover design! Shari Reinhart for your valuable insights throughout the editing process.

Last, but never least…Family and Friends. Curtis, Mike, Diane, Kendra, Salina and Luis, and the boys. Jamie and Lorraine. Chris, both Senior and Junior. Todd. Tim. Clay. Tara. Keanue. Paul. MJ. Rex. Susan. Julie. Fairbourne. Dylan. Carolyn. Lisa. Landon and Ash. Words are not enough. Thank you for holding space for me. For your encouragement. For your love.

puz·zle [pəzəl/]

Verb

1. Cause (someone) to feel confused because they cannot understand or make sense of something

a. *Synonym*: perplex, confuse, bewilder, bemuse, baffle, mystify, confound

Noun

2. A game, toy, or problem designed to test ingenuity or knowledge

BIOGRAPHY

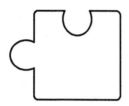

Linda Green served 32 years with the California Department of Forestry & Fire Prevention. She held the ranks of Firefighter I, Fire Apparatus Engineer, Fire Captain, Battalion Chief and Assistant Chief. She served 10 years on Incident Management Teams and was an Adjunct Instructor at CAL FIRE's Academy for Basic Fire Control academies, providing ongoing training at the local, regional and state level, including 15 yrs on the S-420 cadre for Command & General Staff.

She holds a B.A. in Business Management from the University of Phoenix and an A.S. Fire Science from Fresno City College. She was the camp commander for the Delta Conservation Camp. And before that, worked in the Cobb area as both a Fire Captain and Battalion Chief for over 12 years. She was the Class Coordinator and driving force behind the Colusa County Fire Academy #1, a joint effort with Colusa County Office of Education, CAL FIRE and local fire agencies. She was awarded the Department Commendation for participating in a research project to develop improved safety apparel. She volunteers at the First Responder Support Network/ West Coast Post Traumatic Retreat as a Peer (First Responder). Their mission is to provide educational treatment programs to promote recovery from stress and critical incidents experienced by first responders and their families.

With her broadened spectrum of service as a writer, author and Certified High Performance Coach, she uses her strategic principles and wisdom to guide other First Responders through the discovery process with unique puzzle-solving strategies pre and post diagnosis to create their own recovery roadmap. Linda and her husband Curtis recently celebrated their 31st wedding anniversary and live in a quiet town in northern California with two dogs.

CPSIA information can be obtained
at www.ICGtesting.com
Printed in the USA
LVHW021209071019
633402LV00001B/76/P

9 781724 878816